The Battle of Agincourt by Michael Drayton

Michael Drayton was born in 1563 at Hartshill, near Nuneaton, Warwickshire, England. The facts of his early life remain unknown.

Drayton first published, in 1590, a volume of spiritual poems; The Harmony of the Church. Ironically the Archbishop of Canterbury seized almost the entire edition and had it destroyed.

In 1593 he published Idea: The Shepherd's Garland, 9 pastorals celebrating his own love-sorrows under the poetic name of Rowland. This was later expanded to a 64 sonnet cycle.

With the publication of The Legend of Piers Gaveston, Matilda and Mortimeriados, later enlarged and re-published, in 1603, under the title of The Barons' Wars. His career began to gather interest and attention.

In 1596, The Legend of Robert, Duke of Normandy, another historical poem was published, followed in 1597 by England's Heroical Epistles, a series of historical studies, in imitation of those of Ovid. Written in the heroic couplet, they contain some of his finest writing.

Like other poets of his era, Drayton wrote for the theatre; but unlike Shakespeare, Jonson, or Samuel Daniel, he invested little of his art in the genre. Between 1597 and 1602, Drayton was a member of the stable of playwrights who worked for Philip Henslowe. Henslowe's Diary links Drayton's name with 23 plays from that period, and, for all but one unfinished work, in collaboration with others such as Thomas Dekker, Anthony Munday, and Henry Chettle. Only one play has survived; Part 1 of Sir John Oldcastle, which Drayton wrote with Munday, Robert Wilson, and Richard Hathwaye but little of Drayton can be seen in its pages.

By this time, as a poet, Drayton was well received and admired at the Court of Elizabeth 1st. If he hoped to continue that admiration with the accession of James 1st he thought wrong. In 1603, he addressed a poem of compliment to James I, but it was ridiculed, and his services rudely rejected.

In 1605 Drayton reprinted his most important works; the historical poems and the Idea. Also published was a fantastic satire called The Man in the Moon and, for the for the first time the famous Ballad of Agincourt.

Since 1598 he had worked on Poly-Olbion, a work to celebrate all the points of topographical or antiquarian interest in Great Britain. Eighteen books in total, the first were published in 1614 and the last in 1622.

In 1627 he published another of his miscellaneous volumes. In it Drayton printed The Battle of Agincourt (an historical poem but not to be confused with his ballad on the same subject), The Miseries of Queen Margaret, and the acclaimed Nimphidia, the Court of Faery, as well as several other important pieces.

Drayton last published in 1630 with The Muses' Elizium.

Michael Drayton died in London on December 23rd, 1631. He was buried in Westminster Abbey, in Poets' Corner. A monument was placed there with memorial lines attributed to Ben Jonson.

Index of Contents

INTRODUCTION by Richard Garnett

All civilized nations possessing a history which they contemplate with pride endeavour to present that history in an epic form. In their initial stages of culture the vehicles of expression are ballads like the constituents of the Spanish Romanceros and chronicles like Joinville's and Froissart's. With literary refinement comes the distinct literary purpose, and the poet appears who is also more or less of an artist. The number of Spanish and Portuguese national epics, from the Lusiad downwards, during the sixteenth and the first half of the seventeenth centuries, is astonishing; and it was impossible that English authorship, rapidly acquiring a perception of literary form under classical and foreign influences, should not be powerfully affected by the example of its neighbours.

A remarkable circumstance, nevertheless, while encouraging this epical impulse, deprived its most important creations of the external epical form. The age of awakened national self-consciousness was also the age of drama. The greatest poetical genius of that or any age, and his associates, were playwrights first and poets afterwards. The torrent of inspiration rushed mainly to the stage. Hence the old experience was reversed, and whereas Æschylus described himself and his fellow-dramatists as subsisting on scraps filched from the great banquet of Homer, our English epic poets could but follow humbly in the wake of the dramatists, the alchemy of whose genius had already turned the dross of ancient chronicles to gold. In the mighty series of Shakespeare's historical plays, including in the enumeration Marlowe's "Edward the Second" and the anonymous "Edward the Third," England possesses a national epic inferior to that of no country in the world, although the form be dramatic. In one respect, indeed, this epic is superior to any but the Homeric poems, standing one remove less apart from the poetry of the people. The impression of primitive force which the Homeric poems convey by their venerable language is equally well imparted by Shakespeare's spontaneity and his apparent and probably real innocence of all purely literary intention.

Epic poets, however gifted, could be but gleaners after such a harvest. Yet not every excellent poet, even of that dramatic age, was endowed with the dramatic faculty, and two of especial merit, singularly devoid of dramatic gift, but inferior to none in love of their country and self-consecration to its service, turned their attention to the epic. These were Samuel Daniel and Michael Drayton. The latter is our subject, but something should also be said of the former. Drayton not unfairly hit the blot in his successful rival when he said of him:

"His rimes were smooth, his meeters well did close,
But yet his maner better fitted prose."

This is one way of putting it; from another point of view Daniel may be regarded as almost the most remarkable literary phenomenon of his time; he is so exceedingly modern. He outran the taste of his own period by a hundred years, and without teacher or example displayed the excellences which came to be preferred to all others in the eighteenth century. "These poems of his," says his editor in that age (1718), "having stood the test of above a century, and the language and the versification being still pure and elegant, it is to be hoped they will still shine among his countrymen and preserve his name." At this time, and for long afterwards, Drayton, save for an occasional reprint of his "Nimphidia" among miscellaneous collections, was utterly neglected. Even after the editions of 1748 and 1753 he is alluded to by Goldsmith as a type of the poet whose best title to fame is his tomb in Westminster Abbey. The nineteenth century has reversed this with other critical verdicts of the eighteenth, and, with all due respect to Daniel, Drayton now stands higher. Yet, where the two poets come most directly and manifestly into competition, Drayton's superiority is not so evident. As a whole, Daniel's "Civil War" is a better poem than Drayton's "Barons' Wars." The superiority of the latter lies in particular passages, such as the description of the guilty happiness of Isabella and Mortimer, quoted in Mr. Arthur Bullen's admirable selection. This is to say that Drayton's genius was naturally not so much epical as lyrical and descriptive. In his own proper business as a narrative poet he fails as compared with Daniel, but he enriches history with all the ornaments of poetry; and it was his especial good fortune to discover a subject in which the union of dry fact with copious poetic illustration was as legitimate to the theme as advantageous to the writer. This was, of course, his "Poly-Olbion," where, doing for himself what no other poet ever did, he did for his country what was never done for any other. Greece and Rome, indeed, have left us versified topographies, but these advance no pretension to the poetical character except from the metrical point of view, though they may in a sense claim kinship with the Muses as the manifest offspring of Mnemosyne. If any modern language possesses a similar work, it has failed to inscribe itself on the roll of the world's literature. The difficulties of Drayton's unique undertaking were in a measure favourable to him. They compelled him to exert his fancy to the uttermost. The tremendous difficulty of making topography into poetry gave him unwonted energy. He never goes to sleep, as too often in the "Barons' Wars." The stiff practical obstacles attendant upon the poetical treatment of towns and rivers provoke even the dragging Alexandrine into animation; his stream is often all foam and eddy. The long sweeping line, of its wont so lumbering and tedious, is perfectly in place here. It rushes along like an impetuous torrent, bearing with it, indeed, no inconsiderable quantity of wood, hay, and stubble, but also precious pearls, and more than the dust of gold. Its "swelling and limitless billows" mate well with the amplitude of the subject, so varied and spacious that, as has been well said, the "Poly-Olbion" is not a poem to be read through, but to be read in. Nothing in our literature, perhaps, except the "Faery Queen," more perfectly satisfies Keats's desideratum: "Do not the lovers of poetry like to have a little region to wander in, where they may pick and choose, and in which the images are so numerous that many are forgotten and found new in a second reading: which may be food for a week's stroll in the summer? Do they not like this better than what they can read through before Mrs. Williams comes down stairs? a morning work at most?"

The "Poly-Olbion" was completed by 1619, though the concluding part was not published until 1623. "The Battaile of Agincourt," the poem now reprinted, appeared with others in 1627. As none of the pieces comprised in it had appeared in the collected edition of Drayton's works (the "Poly-Olbion" excepted) which he had published in 1620, it is reasonable to conclude that they had been composed between that date and 1627. They prove that his powers were by no means abated. "Nimphidia," in particular, though lacking the exquisite sweetness of some of his lyric pastorals, and the deep emotion of passages in his "Heroicall Epistles," excels all his other productions in airy fancy, and is perhaps the best known of any of his poems. Nor does the "Battaile" itself indicate any decay in poetical power, though we must agree with Mr. Bullen that it is in some parts fatiguing. This wearisomeness proceeds chiefly from Drayton's over-faithful adherence, not so much to the actual story, as to the method of the chronicler from whom his materials are principally drawn. It does not seem to have occurred to him to regard his theme in the light of potter's clay. Following his authority with servile deference, he makes at the beginning a slip which lowers the dignity of his hero, and consequently of his epic. He represents Henry the Fifth's expedition against France as originally prompted, not by the restless enterprise and fiery valour of the young king, much less by supernatural inspiration as the working out of a divine purpose, but by the craft of the clergy seeking to divert him from too nice inquiry into the source and application of their revenues. Henry, therefore, without, as modern investigators think, even sufficient historical authority, but in any case without poetical justification, appears at the very beginning of the poem that celebrates his exploits in the light of a dupe. Shakespeare avoids this awkwardness by boldly altering the date of Henry's embassy to France. His play opens, indeed, with the plots of the ecclesiastics to tempt the king into war, but it soon appears that the embassy claiming certain French dukedoms has been despatched before they had opened their lips, and that they are urging him to a course of action on which he is resolved already. Spenser or Dryden would have escaped from the difficulty in a manner more in accordance with epic precedent by representing Henry's action as the effect of a divine vision. Edward the Third or the Black Prince would have risen from the grave to urge him to renew and complete their interrupted and now almost undone work; or the ghosts of chiefs untimely slain would have reproached him with their abandoned conquests and neglected graves. Drayton has merely taken the story as he found it, without a thought of submitting its dross to the alchemy of the re-creative imagination of the poet. The same lack of selection is observable in his description of the battle itself. He minutely describes a series of episodes, in themselves often highly picturesque, but we are no better able to view the conflict as a whole than if we ourselves had fought in the ranks. As in painting, so in poetry, a true impression is not to be conveyed by microscopic accuracy in minutiæ, but by a vigorous grasp of the entire subject.

Notwithstanding these defects, which one might have thought would have been avoided even by a poet endowed with less of the bright and sprightly invention which Drayton manifests in so many of his pieces, "The Battaile of Agincourt" is a fine poem, and well deserving the honour of reprint. It is above all things patriotic, pervaded throughout by a manly and honourable preference for England and all things English, yet devoid of bitterness towards the enemy, whose valour is frankly acknowledged, and whose overweening pride, the cause of their disasters, is never made the object of ill-natured sarcasm. It may almost be said that if Drayton had been in some respects a worse man, he might on this occasion have been a better poet. He is so sedulously regardful of the truth of history, or what he takes to be such, that he neglects the poet's prerogative of making history, and rises and falls with his model like a moored vessel pitching in a flowing tide. When his historical authority inspires, Drayton is inspired accordingly; when it is dignified, so is he; with it he soars and sings, with it he also sinks and creeps. Happily the subject is usually picturesque, and old Holinshed at his worst was no contemptible writer. Drayton's heart too was in his work, as he had proved long before by the noble ballad on King Harry reprinted in this volume. If he has not shown himself an artist in the selection and arrangement of his topics, he deserves the name from another point of view by the excellent metrical structure of his octaves, and the easy fluency of his narrative. One annoying defect, the frequent occurrence of flat single lines not far remote from bathos, must be attributed to the low standard of the most refined poetry in an age when "the judges and police of literature" had hardly begun either to make laws or to enforce them. It is a fault which he shared with most others, and of which he has himself given more offensive instances. It is still more conspicuous in the most generally acceptable of his poems, the "Nimphidia." The pity is not so much the occasional occurrence of such lapses in "The Battaile of Agincourt," as the want of those delightful touches in the other delightful poems which give more pleasure the more evidently they are embellishments rather springing out of the author's fancy than naturally prompted by his subject. Such are the lines, as inappropriate in the mouth of the speaker as genuine from the heart of the writer, near the beginning of Queen Margaret's epistle to the Duke of Suffolk ("England's Heroicall Epistles"):

"The little bird yet to salute the morn
Upon the naked branches sets her foot,
The leaves then lying on the mossy root,
And there a silly chirruping doth keep,
As if she fain would sing, yet fain would weep;
Praising fair summer that too soon is gone,
Or sad for winter too soon coming on."

On a more exact comparison of Drayton with Holinshed we find him omitting some circumstances which he might have been expected to have retained, and adding others with good judgment and in general with good effect, but which by some fatality usually tend in his hands to excessive prolixity. This is certainly not the case with his dignified and spirited exordium, but in the fourth stanza he begins to copy history, and his muse's wing immediately flags. No more striking example of the superiority of dramatic to narrative poetry in vividness of delineation could be found than the contrast between Shakespeare's scene representing the Archbishop of Canterbury and the Bishop of Ely in actual conversation, and Drayton's tame exposition of the outcome of their deliberations. In his report of the session of Parliament where the French war is discussed he closely follows Holinshed, so closely as to omit Shakespeare's masterly embellishment of Henry's solemn appeal to the Archbishop to pronounce on the justice of his cause as in the sight of God. Drayton must assuredly have perceived how greatly such an appeal tended to exalt his hero's character, and what an opening it afforded for impressive rhetoric. Nor could the incident have escaped his notice, for there is abundant internal evidence of his acquaintance with Shakespeare's drama in the closet as well as on the stage. It can only be concluded that he did not choose to be indebted to Shakespeare, or despaired of rivalling him. His notice of his great contemporary in the "Epistle to Reynolds" is surprisingly cold; but the legend, however unauthentic, of Shakespeare's death from a fever contracted at a merry-making in Drayton's company, seems incompatible with any serious estrangement, and Shakespeare's son-in-law was Drayton's physician when the latter revisited his native Warwickshire. The same jealousy of obligation must have influenced his treatment of the incident of the Dauphin's derisive present of tennis balls, which both Shakespeare and he have adopted from Holinshed or his authorities, but of which the former has made everything and the latter nothing. Nor can the omission of the highly dramatic incident of the conspiracy of Scroop and Cambridge, found in Holinshed, be otherwise well accounted for. In compensation, Drayton introduces two episodes entirely his own, the catalogue of Henry's ships, and that of the armorial ensigns of the British counties. Ben Jonson may be suspected of a sneer when he congratulates Drayton on thus outdoing Homer, as he had previously outdone, or at least rivalled, Virgil, Theocritus, Ovid, Orpheus, and Lucan. Ben might have said with perfect sincerity that Drayton's descriptions are fine pieces of work, showing great command of language, and only open to criticism from some want of proportion between them and the poem of which they are but subordinate episodes. This censure would have been by no means just if the whole piece had been executed on the scale of the description of the siege of Harfleur. It is difficult to imagine what could have tempted Drayton to spend so much time upon an episode treated by Holinshed with comparative brevity. Some of the stanzas are exceedingly spirited, but as a whole the description certainly fatigues. If the same is to some extent the case with the description of the Battle of Agincourt itself, the cause is not so much prolixity as the multitude of separate episodes, not always derived from the chroniclers, and the consequent want of unity which has been already adverted to. The result is probably more true to the actual impression of a battle than if Drayton had surveyed the field with the eye of a tactician, but here as elsewhere the poet should rather aim at an exalted and in some measure idealized representation of the object or circumstance described than at a faithful reproduction of minor details. Even the Battle of the Frogs and Mice in Homer is an orderly whole; while Drayton's battle seems always ending and always beginning anew, a Sisyphian epic. What, however, really kindles and vivifies the unequal composition into one glowing mass is the noble spirit of enthusiastic patriotism which pervades the poet's mind, and, like sunlight in a mountainous tract, illuminates his heights, veils his depressions, and steeps the whole in glory.

Of the literary history of "The Battaile of Agincourt" there is little to be said. It was first published in 1627, along with "Nimphidia," "The Shepheard's Sirena," and others of Drayton's best pieces. It was accompanied by three copies of congratulatory verse, reprinted here, the most remarkable of which is that proceeding from the pen of Ben Jonson, who admits that some had accounted him no friend to Drayton, and whose encomiums are to our apprehension largely flavoured with irony. Drayton, in his "Epistle to Reynolds," which Jonson must have seen, had compared him to Seneca and Plautus,(1) and Jonson seems to burlesque the compliment by comparing Drayton himself to every poet whom he had ever imitated, until his single person seems an epitome of all Parnassus. The poem and its companions had another edition in 1631, since which time it has been included in every edition of Drayton's works, but has never till now been published by itself. Even here it is graced with a satellite, the splendid Ballad of Agincourt ("To my Frinds the Camber-Britans and theyr Harp"), originally published in "Poemes lyric and pastoral," probably about 1605. This stirring strain, always admired, has attracted additional notice in the present day as the metrical prototype of Tennyson's "Charge of the Light Brigade," which, in our estimation, fails to rival its model. The lapses of both poets may well be excused on the ground of the difficulty of the metre, but Drayton has the additional apology of the "brave neglect" which so correct a writer as Pope accounted a virtue in Homer, but which Tennyson never had the nerve to permit himself.

Comparisons between modern and ancient poets must necessarily be very imperfect; yet our Drayton might not inaptly be termed the English Theocritus. If not so distinctly superior to every other English pastoral poet as Theocritus was to every other Greek, he yet stands in the front rank. He is utterly free from affectation, the great vice of pastoral poetry; his love of the country is sincere; his perception of natural phenomena exquisite; his shepherds and shepherdesses real swains and lasses; he has happily varied the conventional form of the pastoral by a felicitous lyrical treatment. Paradoxical as it may appear, Drayton was partly enabled to approach Theocritus so nearly by knowing him so imperfectly. Had he been acquainted with him otherwise than through Virgil, he would probably have been unable to refrain from direct imitation; but as matters stand, instead of a poet striving to write as Theocritus wrote in Greek, we have one actually writing as Theocritus would have written in English. But the most remarkable point of contact between Drayton and Theocritus is that both are epical as well as pastoral poets. Two of the Idylls of Theocritus are believed to be fragments of an epic on the exploits of Hercules; and in the enumeration of his lost works, amid others of the same description, mention is made of the "Heroines," a curious counterpart of Drayton's "Heroicall Epistles." Had these works survived, we might not improbably have found Drayton surpassing his prototype in epic as much as he falls below him in pastoral; for the more exquisite art of the Sicilian could hardly have made amends for the lack of that

national pride and enthusiastic patriotism which had died out of his age, but which ennobled the strength and upbore the weakness of the author of "The Battaile of Agincourt."
Richard Garnett.

(1) *Pope's celebrated verse, —*
"Drink deep, or taste not the Pierian spring,"—
is "conveyed" from this passage of Drayton.

DEDICATION

To you those Noblest of Gentlemen, of these Renowned Kingdomes of Great Britaine: who in these declining times, have yet in your brave bosomes the sparkes of that sprightly fire, of your couragious Ancestors; and to this houre retaine the seedes of their magnanimitie and Greatnesse, who out of the vertue of your mindes, love and cherish neglected Poesie, the delight of Blessed soules, and the language of Angels. To you are these my Poems dedicated,
By your truly affectioned Servant,
Michael Drayton.

UPON THE BATTAILE OF AGINCOURT, WRITTEN BY HIS DEARE FRIEND MICHAEL DRAYTON ESQUIRE

Had Henryes name beene onely met in Prose,
Recorded by the humble wit of those,
Who write of lesse then Kings: who victory,
As calmely mention, as a Pedigree,
The French, alike with us, might view his name
His actions too, and not confesse a shame:
Nay, grow at length, so boldly troublesome,
As, to dispute if they were overcome.
But thou hast wakte their feares: thy fiercer hand
Hath made their shame as lasting, as their land.
By thee againe they are compeld to knowe
How much of Fate is in an English foe.
They bleede afresh by thee, and thinke the harme
Such; they could rather wish, t'were Henryes arme:
Who thankes thy painfull quill; and holds it more
To be thy Subiect now, then King before.
By thee he conquers yet; when ev'ry word
Yeelds him a fuller honour, then his sword.
Strengthens his action against time: by thee,
Hee victory, and France, doth hold in fee.
So well obseru'd he is, that ev'ry thing
Speakes him not onely English, but a King.
And France, in this, may boast her fortunate
That shee was worthy of so brave a hate.

Her suffring is her gayne. How well we see
The Battaile labour'd worthy him, and thee,
Where, wee may Death discover with delight,
And entertaine a pleasure from a fight.
Where wee may see how well it doth become
The brau'ry of a Prince to overcome.
What Power is a Poet: that can add
A life to Kings, more glorious, then they had.
For what of Henry, is unsung by thee,
Henry doth want of his Eternity.
I. Vavghan.

What lofty Trophyes of eternall Fame,
England may vaunt thou do'st erect to her,
Yet forced to confesse, (yea blush for shame,)
That she no Honour doth on thee confer.
How it would become her, would she learne to knowe
Once to requite thy Heaven-borne Art and Zeale,
Or at the least her selfe but thankfull showe
Her ancient Glories that do'st still reueale:
Sing thou of Love, thy straines (like powerfull Charmes)
Enrage the bosome with an amorous fire,
And when againe thou lik'st to sing of Armes
The Coward thou with Courage do'st inspire:
But when thou com'st to touch our Sinfull Times,
Then Heaven far more then Earth speakes in thy Rimes.
John Reynolds.

It hath beene question'd, Michael, if I bee
A Friend at all; or, if at all, to thee:
Because, who make the question, have not seene
Those ambling visits, passe in verse, betweene
Thy Muse, and mine, as they expect. 'Tis true:
You have not writ to me, nor I to you;
And, though I now begin, 'tis not to rub
Hanch against Hanch, or raise a riming Club
About the towne: this reck'ning I will pay,
Without conferring symboles. This 's my day.
It was no Dreame! I was awake, and saw!
Lend me thy voyce, O Fame, that I may draw

Wonder to truth! and have my Vision hoorld,
Hot from thy trumpet, round, about the world.
I saw a Beauty from the Sea to rise,
That all Earth look'd on; and that earth, all Eyes!
It cast a beame as when the chear-full Sun
Is fayre got up, and day some houres begun!
And fill'd an Orbe as circular, as Heaven!
The Orbe was cut forth into Regions seauen.
And those so sweet, and well proportion'd parts,
As it had beene the circle of the Arts!
When, by thy bright Ideas standing by,
I found it pure, and perfect Poesy,
There read I, streight, thy learned Legends three,
Heard the soft ayres, between our Swaynes & thee,
Which made me thinke, the old Theocritus,
Or Rurall Virgil come, to pipe to us!
But then, thy'epistolar Heroick Songs,
Their loves, their quarrels, iealousies, and wrongs
Did all so strike me, as I cry'd, who can
With us be call'd, the Naso, but this man?
And looking up, I saw Mineruas fowle,
Pearch'd over head, the wise Athenian Owle:
I thought thee then our Orpheus, that wouldst try
Like him, to make the ayre, one volary:
And I had stil'd thee, Orpheus, but before
My lippes could forme the voyce, I heard that Rore,
And Rouze, the Marching of a mighty force,
Drums against Drums, the neighing of the Horse,
The Fights, the Cryes, and wondring at the Iarres
I saw, and read, it was thy Barons Warres!
O, how in those, dost thou instruct these times,
That Rebells actions, are but valiant crimes!
And caried, though with shoute, and noyse, confesse
A wild, and an authoriz'd wickednesse!
Sayst thou so, Lucan? But thou scornst to stay
Under one title. Thou hast made thy way
And flight about the Ile, well neare, by this,
In thy admired Periégesis,
Or uniuersall circumduction
Of all that reade thy Poly-Olbyon.
That reade it? that are rauish'd! such was I
With every song, I sweare, and so would dye:
But that I heare, againe, thy Drum to beate
A better cause, and strike the bravest heate
That euer yet did fire the English blood!
Our right in France! if ritely understood.
There, thou art Homer! Pray thee use the stile
Thou hast deserv'd: And let me reade the while

Thy Catalogue of Ships, exceeding his,
Thy list of aydes, and force, for so it is:
The Poets act! and for his Country's sake
Brave are the Musters, that the Muse will make.
And when he ships them where to use their Armes,
How do his trumpets breath! What loud alarmes!
Looke, how we read the Spartans were inflam'd
With bold Tyrtæus verse, when thou art nam'd,
So shall our English Youth vrge on, and cry
An Agincourt, an Agincourt, or dye.
This booke! it is a Catechisme to fight,
And will be bought of every Lord, and Knight,
That can but reade; who cannot, may in prose
Get broken peeces, and fight well by those.
The miseries of Margaret the Queene
Of tender eyes will more be wept, then seene:
I feele it by mine owne, that over flow,
And stop my sight, in every line I goe.
But then refreshed, with thy Fayerie Court,
I looke on Cynthia, and Sirenas sport,
As, on two flowry Carpets, that did rise,
And with their grassie greene restor'd mine eyes.
Yet give mee leaue, to wonder at the birth
Of thy strange Moon-Calfe, both thy straine of mirth,
And Gossip-got acquaintance, as, to us
Thou hadst brought Lapland, or old Cobalus,
Empusa, Lamia, or some Monster, more
Then Affricke knew, or the full Grecian shore!
I gratulate it to thee, and thy Ends,
To all thy vertuous, and well chosen Friends,
Onely my losse is, that I am not there:
And, till I worthy am to wish I were,
I call the world, that enuies mee, to see
If I can be a Friend, and Friend to thee.

THE BATTLE OF AGINCOURT

Ceas'd was the Thunder, of those Drummes which wak'd
Th'affrighted French their miseries to view,
At Edwards name, which to that houre still quak'd,
Their Salique Tables to the ground that threw,
Yet were the English courages not slak'd,
But the same Bowes, and the same Blades they drew,
With the same Armes, those weapons to aduance,
Which lately lopt the Flower de liz of France.

Wonder to truth! and have my Vision hoorld,
Hot from thy trumpet, round, about the world.
I saw a Beauty from the Sea to rise,
That all Earth look'd on; and that earth, all Eyes!
It cast a beame as when the chear-full Sun
Is fayre got up, and day some houres begun!
And fill'd an Orbe as circular, as Heaven!
The Orbe was cut forth into Regions seauen.
And those so sweet, and well proportion'd parts,
As it had beene the circle of the Arts!
When, by thy bright Ideas standing by,
I found it pure, and perfect Poesy,
There read I, streight, thy learned Legends three,
Heard the soft ayres, between our Swaynes & thee,
Which made me thinke, the old Theocritus,
Or Rurall Virgil come, to pipe to us!
But then, thy'epistolar Heroick Songs,
Their loves, their quarrels, iealousies, and wrongs
Did all so strike me, as I cry'd, who can
With us be call'd, the Naso, but this man?
And looking up, I saw Mineruas fowle,
Pearch'd over head, the wise Athenian Owle:
I thought thee then our Orpheus, that wouldst try
Like him, to make the ayre, one volary:
And I had stil'd thee, Orpheus, but before
My lippes could forme the voyce, I heard that Rore,
And Rouze, the Marching of a mighty force,
Drums against Drums, the neighing of the Horse,
The Fights, the Cryes, and wondring at the Iarres
I saw, and read, it was thy Barons Warres!
O, how in those, dost thou instruct these times,
That Rebells actions, are but valiant crimes!
And caried, though with shoute, and noyse, confesse
A wild, and an authoriz'd wickednesse!
Sayst thou so, Lucan? But thou scornst to stay
Under one title. Thou hast made thy way
And flight about the Ile, well neare, by this,
In thy admired Periégesis,
Or uniuersall circumduction
Of all that reade thy Poly-Olbyon.
That reade it? that are rauish'd! such was I
With every song, I sweare, and so would dye:
But that I heare, againe, thy Drum to beate
A better cause, and strike the bravest heate
That euer yet did fire the English blood!
Our right in France! if ritely understood.
There, thou art Homer! Pray thee use the stile
Thou hast deserv'd: And let me reade the while

Thy Catalogue of Ships, exceeding his,
Thy list of aydes, and force, for so it is:
The Poets act! and for his Country's sake
Brave are the Musters, that the Muse will make.
And when he ships them where to use their Armes,
How do his trumpets breath! What loud alarmes!
Looke, how we read the Spartans were inflam'd
With bold Tyrtæus verse, when thou art nam'd,
So shall our English Youth vrge on, and cry
An Agincourt, an Agincourt, or dye.
This booke! it is a Catechisme to fight,
And will be bought of every Lord, and Knight,
That can but reade; who cannot, may in prose
Get broken peeces, and fight well by those.
The miseries of Margaret the Queene
Of tender eyes will more be wept, then seene:
I feele it by mine owne, that over flow,
And stop my sight, in every line I goe.
But then refreshed, with thy Fayerie Court,
I looke on Cynthia, and Sirenas sport,
As, on two flowry Carpets, that did rise,
And with their grassie greene restor'd mine eyes.
Yet give mee leaue, to wonder at the birth
Of thy strange Moon-Calfe, both thy straine of mirth,
And Gossip-got acquaintance, as, to us
Thou hadst brought Lapland, or old Cobalus,
Empusa, Lamia, or some Monster, more
Then Affricke knew, or the full Grecian shore!
I gratulate it to thee, and thy Ends,
To all thy vertuous, and well chosen Friends,
Onely my losse is, that I am not there:
And, till I worthy am to wish I were,
I call the world, that enuies mee, to see
If I can be a Friend, and Friend to thee.

THE BATTLE OF AGINCOURT

Ceas'd was the Thunder, of those Drummes which wak'd
Th'affrighted French their miseries to view,
At Edwards name, which to that houre still quak'd,
Their Salique Tables to the ground that threw,
Yet were the English courages not slak'd,
But the same Bowes, and the same Blades they drew,
With the same Armes, those weapons to aduance,
Which lately lopt the Flower de liz of France.

Henry the fift, that man made out of fire,
Th'Imperiall Wreath plac'd on his Princely browe;
His Lyons courage stands not to enquire
Which way olde Henry came by it; or howe
At Pomfret Castell Richard should expire:
What's that to him? He hath the Garland now;
Let Bullingbrook beware how he it wan,
For Munmouth meanes to keepe it, if he can.

That glorious day, which his great Father got,
Upon the Percyes; calling to their ayde
The valiant Dowglass, that Herculian Scot,
When for his Crowne at Shrewsbury they playde,
Had quite dishartned ev'ry other plot,
And all those Tempests quietly had layde,
That not a cloud did to this Prince appeare,
No former King had seene a skye so cleere.

Yet the rich Clergy felt a fearefull Rent,
In the full Bosome of their Church (whilst she
A Monarchesse, immeasurably spent,
Lesse then she was, and thought she might not be:)
By Wickclif and his followers; to preuent
The growth of whose opinions, and to free
That foule Aspersion, which on her they layde,
She her strongst witts must stirre up to her ayde.

When presently a Parliament is calld
To sett things steddy, that stood not so right,
But that thereby the poore might be inthral'd,
Should they be vrged by those that were of might,
That in his Empire, equitie enstauld,
It should continue in that perfect plight;
Wherefore to Lester, he th'Assembly drawes,
There to Inact those necessary Lawes.

In which one Bill (mongst many) there was red,
Against the generall, and superfluous waste
Of temporall Lands, (the Laity that had fed)
Upon the Houses of Religion caste,
Which for defence might stand the Realme in sted,
Where it most needed were it rightly plac't;
Which made those Church-men generally to feare,
For all this calme, some tempest might be neare.

And being right skilfull, quickly they forsawe,
No shallow braines this bus'nesse went about:
Therefore with cunning they must cure this flawe;

For of the King they greatly stood in doubt,
Lest him to them, their opposites should drawe,
Some thing must be thrust in, to thrust that out:
And to this end they wisely must provide
One, this great Engine, Clearkly that could guide.

Chichley, that sate on Canterburies See,
A man well spoken, grauely stout, and wise,
The most select, (then thought of that could be,)
To act what all the Prelacie diuise;
(For well they knew, that in this bus'nesse, he
Would to the vtmost straine his faculties;)
Him lift they up, with their maine strength, to prove
By some cleane slight this Lybell to remove.

His braine in labour, gladly foorth would bring
Somewhat, that at this needfull time might fit,
The sprightly humor of this youthfull King,
If his inuention could but light of it;
His working soule proiecteth many a thing,
Untill at length out of the strength of wit,
He found a warre with France, must be the way
To dash this Bill, else threatning their decay.

Whilst vacant mindes sate in their breasts at ease,
And the remembrance of their Conquests past,
Upon their fansies doth so strongly sease,
As in their teeth, their Cowardise it cast
Rehearsing to them those victorious daies,
The deeds of which, beyond their names should last,
That after ages, reading what was theirs,
Shall hardly thinke, those men had any Heires.

And to this point, premeditating well,
A speech, (which chanc'd, the very pinne to cleaue)
Aym'd, whatsoeuer the successe befell
That it no roomth should for a second leaue,
More of this Title then in hand to tell,
If so his skill him did not much deceaue,
And gainst the King in publike should appeare;
Thus frames his speech to the Assembly there.

Pardon my boldnesse, my Liedge Soveraine Lord,
Nor your Dread presence let my speech offend,
Your milde attention, fauourably affoord,
Which, such cleere vigour to my spirit shall lend,
That it shall set an edge upon your Sword,
To my demand, and make you to attend,

Asking you, why, men train'd to Armes you keepe,
Your right in France yet suffering still to sleepe.

Can such a Prince be in an Iland pent,
And poorely thus shutt up within a Sea.
When as your right includes that large extent,
To th'either Alpes your Empire forth to lay,
Can he be English borne, and is not bent
To follow you, appoint you but the way,
Weele wade if we want ships, the waues or climme,
In one hand hold our swords, with th'other swim.

What time controules, your brave great Grandsires claim,
To th'Realme of France, from Philip nam'd the faire,
Which to King Edward by his mother came,
Queene Isabel; that Philips onely heire,
Which this short intermission doth not maime,
But if it did, as he, so yours repaire;
That where his Right in bloud preuailed not,
In spight of hell, yet by his Sword he got.

What set that Conqueror, by their Salique Lawes,
Those poore decrees their Parliaments could make,
He entred on the iustnesse of his Cause,
To make good, what he dar'd to undertake,
And once in Action, he stood not to pause,
But in upon them like a Tempest brake,
And downe their buildings with such fury bare,
That they from mists dissolved were to ayre.

As those brave Edwards, Father, and the Sonne,
At Conquer'd Cressy, with successefull lucke,
Where first all France (as at one game) they wonne,
Neuer two Warriours, such a Battaile strucke,
That when the bloudy dismall fight was done,
Here in one heape, there in another Rucke
Princes and Peasants lay together mixt,
The English Swords, no difference knew betwixt.

There Lewes King of Beame was overthrowne
With valient Charles, of France the younger Brother,
A Daulphine, and two Dukes, in pieces hewen;
To them six Earles lay slaine by one another;
There the grand Prior of France, fetcht his last groane,
Two Archbishops the boystrous Croud doth smother,
There fifteene thousand of their Gentrie dy'de
With each two Souldiers, slaughtered by his side.

Nor the Blacke Prince, at Poyteers battaile fought;
Short of his Father, and himselfe before,
Her King and Prince, that prisoners hither brought
From forty thousand weltring in their gore,
That in the Worlds opinion it was thought,
France from that instant could subsist no more,
The Marshall, and the Constable, there slaine
Under the Standard, in that Battaile ta'ne.

Nor is this clayme for women to succeede,
(Gainst which they would your right to France debarre)
A thing so new, that it so much should neede
Such opposition, as though fetcht from farre,
By Pepin this is prov'd, as by a deede,
Deposing Cheldrick, by a fatall warre,
By Blythild dar'd his title to aduance,
Daughter to Clothar, first so nam'd of France.

Hugh Capet, who from Charles of Lorayne tooke
The Crowne of France, that he in peace might raigne,
As heire to Lingard to her title stooke,
Who was the daughter of King Charlemaine,
So holy Lewes poring on his booke,
Whom that Hugh Capet made his heire againe,
From Ermingard his Grandame, claim'd the Crowne,
Duke Charles his daughter, wrongfully put downe.

Nor thinke my Leege a fitter time then this,
You could have found your Title to aduance,
At the full height when now the faction is,
T'wixt Burgoyne, and the house of Orleance,
Your purpose you not possibly can misse,
It for my Lord so luckily doth chance,
That whilst these two in opposition stand,
You may have time, your Army there to land.

And if my fancy doe not overpresse,
My visuall sence, me thinkes in every eye
I see such cheere, as of our good successe
In France hereafter seemes to Prophecie;
Thinke not my Soveraigne, my Alegeance lesse
Quoth he; my Lords nor doe you misaply
My words: thus long upon this subiect spent,
Who humbly here submit to your assent.

This speech of his, that powerfull Engine prov'd,
Then e'r our Fathers got, which rais'd us hier,
The Clergies feare that quietly remov'd,

And into France transferd our Hostile fier,
It made the English through the world belov'd,
That durst to those so mighty things aspire,
And gaue so cleere a luster to our fame,
That neighbouring Nations trembled at our name.

When through the house, this rumor scarcely ran,
That warre with France propounded was againe,
In all th'Assembly there was not a man,
But put the proiect on with might and maine,
So great applause it generally wan,
That else no bus'nesse they would entertaine,
As though their honour vtterly were lost,
If this designe should any way be crost.

So much mens mindes, now upon France were set
That every one doth with himselfe forecast,
What might fall out this enterprize to let,
As what againe might give it wings of hast,
And for they knew, the French did still abet
The Scot against us, (which we usde to tast)
It question'd was if it were fit or no,
To Conquer them, ere we to France should goe.

Which Ralph then Earle of Westmorland propos'd,
Quoth he, with Scotland let us first begin,
By which we are upon the North inclos'd,
And lockt with us, one Continent within,
Then first let Scotland be by us dispos'd,
And with more ease, yee spatious France may winne,
Else of our selves, ere we our Ships can cleere,
To land in France; they will inuade us here.

Not so brave Neuill, Excester replies,
For that of one two labours were to make,
For Scotland wholly upon France relies;
First, Conquer France, and Scotland yee may take,
Tis the French pay, the Scot to them that tyes,
That stopt, asunder quickly yee shall shake
The French and Scots; to France then first say I,
First, first, to France, then all the Commons cry.

And instantly an Embassy is sent,
To Charles of France, to will him to restore
Those Territories, of whose large extent,
The English Kings were owners of before;
Which if he did not, and incontinent,
The King would set those English on his Shore,

That in despight of him, and all his might,
Should leaue their lives there, or redeeme his right.

First Normandy, in his demand he makes,
With Aquitane, a Dutchy no lesse great,
Aniou, and Mayne, with Gascoyne which he takes
Cleerely his owne, as any English seat;
With these proud France, he first of all awakes,
For their delivery, giuing power to treat;
For well he knew, if Charles should these restore,
No King of France was euer left so poore.

The King, and Daulphin, to his proud demand,
That he might see they no such matter ment,
As a thing fitter for his youthfull hand;
A Tunne of Paris Tennis balls him sent,
Better himselfe to make him understand,
Deriding his ridiculous intent:
And that was all the answere he could get,
Which more, the King doth to this Conquest whet.

That answering the Ambassadour, quoth he,
Thanks for my Balls, to Charles your Soueraigne give,
And thus assure him, and his sonne from me,
I'le send him Balls and Rackets if I live,
That they such Racket shall in Paris see,
When over lyne with Bandies I shall driue,
As that before the Set be fully done,
France may (perhaps) into the Hazard runne.

So little doth luxurious France fore-see
By her disdaine, what shee upon her drew:
In her most bravery seeming then to be,
The punishment that shortly should ensue,
Which so incenst the English King, that he
For full reuenge into that fury grew:
That those three horrors, Famine, Sword, and Fire,
Could not suffice to satisfie his ire.

In all mens mouthes now was no word but warre,
As though no thing had any other name;
And folke would aske of them ariu'd from farre,
What forces were preparing whence they came?
'Gainst any bus'nesse 'twas a lawfull barre
To say for France they were; and 'twas a shame
For any man to take in hand to doe
Ought, but some thing that did belong thereto.

Olde Armours are drest up, and new are made;
Iacks are in working, and strong shirts of Male,
He scowers an olde Fox, he a Bilbowe blade,
Now Shields and Targets onely are for sale;
Who works for warre, now thriueth by his Trade,
The browne Bill, and the Battell-Axe preuaile:
The curious Fletcher fits his well-strung Bowe,
And his barb'd Arrow which he sets to showe.

Tents and Pavillions in the fields are pitcht,
(E'r full wrought up their Roomthynesse to try)
Windowes, and Towers, with Ensignes are inricht,
With ruffling Banners, that doe brave the sky,
Wherewith the wearied Labourer bewitcht
To see them thus hang wauing in his eye:
His toylsome burthen from his back doth throwe,
And bids them worke that will, to France hee'll goe.

Rich Saddles for the Light-horse and the Bard
For to be brau'st there's not a man but plyes,
Plumes, Bandroules, and Caparizons prepar'd;
Whether of two, and men at Armes diuise
The Greaues, or Guyses were the surer guard,
The Vambrasse, or the Pouldron, they should prize;
And where a stand of Pykes plac't close, or large,
Which way to take aduantage in the Charge.

One traynes his Horse, another trayles his Pyke,
He with his Pole-Axe, practiseth the fight,
The Bowe-man (which no Country hath the like)
With his sheafe Arrow, proveth by his might,
How many score off, he his Foe can strike,
Yet not to draw aboue his bosomes hight:
The Trumpets sound the Charge and the Retreat,
The bellowing Drumme, the Martch againe doth beat.

Cannons upon their Caridge mounted are,
Whose Battery France must feele upon her Walls,
The Engineer providing the Petar,
To breake the strong Percullice, and the Balls,
Of Wild-fire deuis'd to throw from farre,
To burne to ground their Pallaces and Halls:
Some studying are, the scale which they had got,
Thereby to take the Leuell of their Shot.

The man in yeares preacht to his youthfull sonne
Prest to this Warre, as they sate by the fire,
What deedes in France were by his Father done,

To this attempt to worke him to aspire,
And told him, there how he an Ensigne wonne,
Which many a yeare was hung up in the Quire:
And in the Battell, where he made his way,
How many French men he struck downe that day.

The good old man, with teares of joy would tell,
In Cressy field what prizes Edward play'd,
As what at Poycteers the Black Prince befell,
How like a Lyon, he about him layd:
In deedes of Armes how Awdley did excell,
For their olde sinnes, how they the French men payd:
How bravely Basset did behave him there:
How Oxford charg'd the Van, Warwick the Reare.

And Boy, quoth he, I have heard thy Grandsire say,
That once he did an English Archer see,
Who shooting at a French twelue score away,
Quite through the body, stuck him to a Tree;
Upon their strengths a King his Crowne might lay:
Such were the men of that brave age, quoth he,
When with his Axe he at his Foe let driue,
Murriain and scalpe downe to the teeth did riue.

The scarlet Judge might now set up his Mule,
With neighing Steeds the Streetes so pestred are;
For where he wont in Westminster to rule,
On his Tribunal sate the man of Warre,
The Lawyer to his Chamber doth recule,
For be hath now no bus'nesse at the Barre:
But to make Wills and Testaments for those
That were for France, their substance to dispose.

By this, the Counsell of this Warre had met,
And had at large of ev'ry thing discust;
And the graue Clergie had with them beene set:
To warrant what they undertook was iust,
And as for monies that to be no let,
They bad the King for that to them to trust:
The Church to pawne, would see her Challice layde,
E'r shee would leaue one Pyoner unpayde.

From Milford Haven, to the mouth of Tweed,
Ships of all burthen to Southampton brought,
For there the King the Rendeuous decreed
To beare aboard his most victorious fraught:
The place from whence he with the greatest speed
Might land in France, (of any that was thought)

And with successe upon that lucky shore,
Where his great Grandsire landed had before.

But, for he found those vessels were to fewe,
That into France his Army should conuay:
He sent to Belgia, whose great store he knewe,
Might now at neede supply him every way.
His bounty ample, as the windes that blewe,
Such Barkes for Portage out of ev'ry bay
In Holland, Zealand, and in Flanders, brings;
As spred the wide sleeve with their canuase wings.

But first seauen Ships from Rochester are sent,
The narrow Seas, of all the French to sweepe:
All men of Warre with scripts of Mart that went,
And had command, the Coast of France to keepe:
The comming of a Navie to preuent,
And view what strength, was in the Bay of Deepe:
And if they found it like to come abroad,
To doe their best to fire it in the Road.

The Bonauenture, George, and the Expence,
Three as tall Ships, as e'r did Cable tewe,
The Henry Royall, at her parting thence,
Like the huge Ruck from Gillingham that flewe:
The Antilop, the Elephant, Defence,
Bottoms as good as euer spread a clue:
All having charge, their voyage having bin,
Before Southampton to take Souldiers in.

Twelue Merchants Ships, of mighty burthen all,
New off the Stocks, that had beene rig'd for Stoad,
Riding in Thames by Lymehouse and Blackwall
That ready were their Merchandize to load,
Straitly commanded by the Admirall,
At the same Port to settle their aboad:
And each of these a Pinnis at command,
To put her fraught conueniently to land.

Eight goodly Ships, so Bristow ready made,
Which to the King they bountifully lent,
With Spanish Wines which they for Ballast lade,
In happy speed of his brave Voyage ment,
Hoping his Conquest should enlarge their Trade,
And there-withall a rich and spacious Tent:
And as, this Fleet the Seuerne Seas doth stem,
Fiue more from Padstowe came along with them.

The Hare of Loo, a right good Ship well knowne,
The yeare before that twice the Strayts had past,
Two wealthy Spanish Merchants did her owne,
Who then but lately had repair'd her wast;
For from her Deck a Pyrate she had blowne,
After a long Fight, and him tooke at last:
And from Mounts Bay sixe more, that still in sight,
Wayted with her before the Ile of Wight.

From Plymmouth next came in the Blazing Starre,
And fiery Dragon to take in their fraught;
With other foure, especiall men of Warre,
That in the Bay of Portugall had fought;
And though returning from a Voyage farre,
Stem'd that rough Sea, when at the high'st it wrought:
With these, of Dertmouth seau'n good Ships there were,
The golden Cressant in their tops that beare.

So Lyme, three Ships into the Nauy sent,
Of which the Sampson scarse a mon'th before,
Had sprung a Planke, and her mayne Mast had spent,
With extreame perill that she got to shore;
With them fiue other out of Waymouth went,
Which by Southampton, were made up a score:
With those that rode (at pleasure) in the Bay,
And that at Anchor before Portsmouth lay.

Next these, Newcastle furnisheth the Fleet
With nine good Hoyes of necessary use;
The Danish Pyrats, valiantly that beet,
Offring to Sack them as they sayl'd for Sluce:
Six Hulks from Hull at Humbers mouth them meet,
Which had them oft accompanied to Pruce.
Fiue more from Yarmouth falling them among,
That had for Fishing beene prepared long.

The Cowe of Harwich, neuer put to flight,
For Hides, and Furres, late to Muscouia bound,
Of the same Port, another nam'd the Spight,
That in her comming lately through the Sound,
After a two-dayes-still-continued fight,
Had made three Flemings runne themselves a ground;
With three neat Flee-boats which with them doe take,
Six Ships of Sandwich up the Fleet to make.

Nine Ships for the Nobility there went,
Of able men, the enterprize to ayde,
Which to the King most liberally they lent,

At their owne charge, and bountifully payde,
Northumberland, and Westmerland in sent
Fourescore at Armes a peece, themselves and layde
At six score Archers each, as Suffolke showes,
Twenty tall men at Armes, with forty Bowes.

Warwick and Stafford leauied at no lesse
Then noble Suffolke, nor doe offer more
Of men at Armes, and Archers which they presse,
Of their owne Tenants, Arm'd with their owne store:
Their forwardnesse fore-showes their good successe
In such a Warre, as had not beene before:
And other Barrons under Earles that were,
Yet dar'd with them an equall charge to beare.

Darcy and Camois, zealous for the King,
Lovell, Fitzwater, Willoughby, and Rosse,
Berckley, Powis, Burrell, fast together cling;
Seymer, and Saint Iohn for the bus'nesse closse,
Each twenty Horse, and forty foote doe bring
More, to nine hundred mounting in the grosse
In those nine Ships, and fitly them bestow'd,
Which with the other fall into the Road.

From Holland, Zeland, and from Flanders wonne
By weekely pay, threescore twelue Bottoms came,
From fifty upward, to fiue hundred Tunne;
For ev'ry use a Marriner could name,
Whose glittering Flags against the Radient Sunne,
Show'd as the Sea had all beene of a flame;
For Skiffes, Crayes, Scallops, and the like, why these
From ev'ry small Creeke, cov'red all the Seas.

The man whose way from London hap'd to lye,
By those he met might guesse the generall force,
Daily encountred as he passed by,
Now with a Troupe of Foote, and then of Horse,
To whom the people still themselves apply,
Bringing them victuals as in mere remorce:
And still the acclamation of the presse,
Saint George for England, to your good successe.

There might a man have seene in ev'ry Streete,
The Father bidding farewell to his Sonne:
Small Children kneeling at their Fathers feete:
The Wife with her deare Husband ne'r had done:
Brother, his Brother, with adieu to greete:
One Friend to take leaue of another runne:

The Mayden with her best belov'd to part,
Gaue him her hand, who tooke away her heart.

The nobler Youth the common ranke aboue,
On their coruetting Coursers mounted faire,
One ware his Mistris Garter, one her Glove;
And he a lock of his deare Ladies haire;
And he her Colours, whom he most did love;
There was not one but did some Fauour weare:
And each one tooke it, on his happy speede,
To make it famous by some Knightly deede.

The cloudes of dust, that from the wayes arose,
Which in their martch, the trampling Troupes doe reare:
When as the Sunne their thicknesse doth oppose
In his descending, shining wondrous cleare,
To the beholder farre off standing showes
Like some besieged Towne, that were on fire:
As though fore-telling e'r they should returne,
That many a Citie yet secure must burne.

The well-rig'd Navie falne into the Road,
For this short Cut with victuall fully stor'd,
The King impatient of their long aboad,
Commands his Army instantly aboard,
Casting to have each Company bestow'd,
As then the time conuenience could afford;
The Ships appointed wherein they should goe,
And Boats prepar'd for waftage to and fro.

To be imbarqu'd when every Band comes downe,
Each in their order as they mustred were,
Or by the difference of their aArmings knowne,
Or by their Colours; for in Ensignes there,
Some wore the Armes of their most ancient Towne,
Others againe their owne Diuises beare,
There was not any, but that more or lesse,
Something had got, that something should expresse.

First, in the Kentish Stremer was a Wood,
Out of whose top an arme that held a Sword,
As their right Embleme; and to make it good,
They aboue other onely had a Word,
Which was; Unconquer'd; as that freest had stood.
cSussex the next that was to come Aboard
Bore a Blacke Lyon Rampant, sore that bled,
With a Field-Arrow darted through the head.

The men of Surrey, Cheeky Blew and gold,
(Which for brave Warren their first Earle they wore,
In many a Field that honour'd was of olde:)
And Hamshere next in the same Colours bore,
Three Lions Passant, th' Armes of Beuis bould,
Who through the World so famous was of yore;
A siluer Tower, Dorsets Red Banner beares;
The Cornishmen two Wrestlers had for theirs.

The Devonshire Band, a Beacon set on fire,
Sommerset a Virgine bathing in a Spring,
Their Cities Armes, the men of Glostershire,
In Gold three Bloudy Cheuernells doe bring;
Wiltshire a Crowned Piramed; As nigher
Then any other to martch to the King;
Barkshire a Stag, under an Oake that stood,
Oxford a White Bull wading in a Flood.

The mustred men for Buckingham, are gone
Under the Swan, the Armes of that olde Towne,
The Londoners, and Middlesex as one,
Are by the Red Crosse, and the Dagger knowne;
The Men of Essex overmatch'd by none,
Under Queene Hellens Image Marching downe;
Suffolke a Sunne halfe risen from the brack,
Norfolke a Triton on a Dolphines backe.

The Souldiers sent from Cambridgshire, a Bay
Upon a Mountaine watred with a shower:
Hartford two Harts that in a Riuer play;
Bedfords an Eagle pearcht upon a Tower,
And Huntington a People proud as they,
Not giuing place to any for their power,
A youthfull Hunter, with a Chaplet Crown'd,
In a pyde Lyam leading forth his Hound.

Northampton with a Castle seated high,
Supported by two Lyons thither came;
The men of Rutland, to them marching nie,
In their rich Ensigne beare an Ermine Ram,
And Lestershire that on their strength relye,
A Bull and Mastiue fighting for the game.
Lincolne a Ship most neatly that was lim'd
In all her Sailes with Flags and Pennons trim'd.

Stout Warwickshire, her ancient badge the Beare,
Worster a Peare-Tree laden with the Fruit,
A Golden Fleece and Hereford doth weare,

Stafford a Hermet in his homely sute,
Shropshire a Falcon towring in the Ayre,
And for the Shiere whose surface seems most brute,
Darby, an Eagle sitting on a Roote,
A swathed Infant holding in her foote.

Olde Nottingham, an Archer clad in greene,
Under a Tree with his drawne Bowe that stood,
Which in a checquer'd Flagge farre off was seene:
It was the Picture of olde Robin Hood,
And Lancashire not as the least I weene,
Thorough three Crownes, three Arrowes smear'd with blood:
Cheshiere a Banner very square and broad,
Wherein a man upon a Lyon rode.

A flaming Lance, the Yorkshiere men for them,
As those for Durham neere againe at hand,
A Myter crowned with a Diadem:
An Armed man, the men of Cumberland:
So Westmerland link'd with it in one Stem,
A Ship that wrackt lay fierd upon the sand:
Northumberland with these com'n as a Brother,
Two Lyons fighting tearing one another.

Thus as themselves the English men had show'd
Under the Ensigne of each sev'rall Shiere,
The Natiue Welch who no lesse honour ow'd
To their owne King, nor yet lesse valiant were,
In one strong Reg'ment had themselves bestow'd,
And of the rest, resumed had the Reare:
To their owne Quarter marching as the rest,
As neatly Arm'd, and bravely as the best.

Pembrooke, a Boat wherein a Lady stood,
Rowing her selfe within a quiet Bay;
Those men of South-Wales of the mixed blood,
Had of the Welch the leading of the way:
Caermardin in her Colours beare a Rood,
Whereon an olde man lean'd himselfe to stay
At a Starre pointing; which of great renowne,
Was skilfull Merlin, namer of that Towne.

Clamorgan men, a Castell great and hie,
From which, out of the Battlement aboue,
A flame shot up it selfe into the skye:
The men of Munmouth (for the ancient love
To that deare Country; neighbouring them so nie)
Next after them in Equipage that move,

Three Crownes Imperiall which supported were,
With three Arm'd Armes, in their proud Ensigne beare.

The men of Brecknock brought a Warlick Tent,
Upon whose top there sate a watchfull Cock,
Radnor, a mountaine of a high assent,
Thereon a Shepheard keeping of his Flock,
As Cardigan the next to them that went,
Came with a Mermayde sitting on a Rock,
And Merioneth beares (as these had done)
Three dancing Goates against the rising Sunne.

Those of Montgomery, beare a prancing Steed,
Denbigh a Neptune with his three-fork'd Mace:
Flintshiere a Workmayd in her Summers weed,
With Sheafe and Sickle (with a warlick pace)
Those of Caernaruon not the least in speed,
Though marching last (in the mayne Armies face)
Three golden Eagles in their Ensigne brought,
Under which oft brave Owen Guyneth fought.

The Seas amazed at the fearefull sight,
Of Armes, and Ensignes, that aboard were brought,
Of Streamers, Banners, Pennons, Ensignes pight,
Upon each Pup and Prowe; and at the fraught,
So full of terror, that it hardly might
Into a naturall course againe be brought,
As the vaste Navie which at Anchor rides,
Proudly presumes to shoulder out the Tides.

The Fleet then full, and floating on the Maine,
The numerous Masts, with their brave Topsailes spred,
When as the Winde a little doth them straine,
Seeme like a Forrest bearing her proud head
Against some rough flawe, that forerunns a raine;
So do they looke from every loftie sted,
Which with the Surges tumbled too and fro,
Seeme (euen) to bend, as trees are seene to doe.

From every Ship when as the Ordnance rore,
Of their depart, that all might understand,
When as the zealous people from the shore,
Againe with fires salute them from the Land,
For so was order left with them before,
To watch the Beacons, with a carefull hand,
Which being once fierd, the people more or lesse,
Should all to Church, and pray for their successe.

They shape their Course into the Month of Seyne,
That destin'd Flood those Navies to receiue,
Before whose fraught her France had prostrate laine,
As now she must this, that shall neuer leaue,
Untill the Engines that it doth containe,
Into the ayre her heightned walls shall heaue;
Whose stubborne Turrets had refus'd to bow,
To that brave Nation that shall shake them now.

Long Boates with Scouts are put to land before,
Upon light Naggs the Countrey to discry,
(Whilst the brave Army setting is on shore,)
To view what strength the enemy had nie,
Pressing the bosome of large France so sore,
That her pale Genius, in affright doth flye
To all her Townes and warnes them to awake,
And for her safety up their Armes to take.

At Paris, Roan, and Orleance, she calls,
And at their gates with gronings doth complaine:
Then cries she out, O get up to your walls:
The English Armies are return'd againe,
Which in two Battailes gaue those fatall falls,
At Cressie, and at Poyteers, where lay slaine
Our conquered Fathers, which with very feare
Quake in their Graves to feele them landed here.

The King of France now having understood,
Of Henries entrance, (but too well improv'd,)
He cleerly saw that deere must be the blood,
That it must cost, e'r he could be remov'd;
He sends to make his other Sea Townes good,
Neuer before so much it him behov'd;
In ev'ry one a Garison to lay,
Fearing fresh powers from England ev'ry day.

To the high'st earth whilst awfull Henry gets,
From whence strong Harflew he might easl'est see,
With sprightly words, and thus their courage whets,
In yonder walls be Mynes of gold (quoth he)
He's a poore Slaue, that thinkes of any debts;
Harflew shall pay for all, it ours shall be:
This ayre of France doth like me wondrous well,
Lets burne our Ships, for here we meane to dwell.

But through his Hoast, he first of all proclaim'd
In paine of death, no English man should take
From the Religious, aged, or the maym'd,

Or women that could no resistance make:
To gaine his owne for that he onely aym'd;
Nor would have such to suffer for his sake:
Which in the French (when they the same did heare)
Bred of this brave King, a religious feare.

His Army rang'd, in order fitting warre,
Each with some greene thing doth his Murrian crowne,
With his mayne standard fixt upon the Carre;
Comes the great King before th'intrenched Towne,
Whilst from the walls the people gazing are,
In all their sights he sets his Army downe;
Nor for their shot he careth not a pin,
But seekes where he his Battery may begin.

And into three, his Army doth diuide,
His strong aproaches on three parts to make;
Himselfe on th'one, Clarence on th'other side,
To Yorke and Suffolke he the third doth take,
The Mines the Duke of Glocester doth guide;
Then caus'd his Ships the Riuer up to Stake,
That none with Victuall should the Towne relieue
Should the Sword faile, with Famine them to grieue.

From his Pavillion where he sate in State,
Arm'd for the Siedge, and buckling on his Shield,
Brave Henry sends his Herault to the Gate,
By Trumpets sound, to summon them to yeeld,
And to accept his Mercy, ere to late,
Or else to say ere he forsooke the field,
Harflew should be but a meere heape of Stones,
Her buildings buried with her Owners bones.

France on this sudaine put into a fright,
With the sad newes of Harflew in distresse,
Whose inexpected, miserable plight,
She on the suddaine, knew not to redresse,
But vrg'd to doe the vtmost that she might,
The peoples feares and clamours to suppresse,
Raiseth a power with all the speede she could,
Somewhat thereby, to loose King Henries hold.

The Marshall, and the Constable of France,
Leading those Forces levied for the turne,
By which they thought their Titles to aduance,
And of their Countrey endlesse praise to earne,
But it with them farre otherwise doth chance,
For when they saw the Villages to burne,

And high-towr'd Harflew round ingirt with fires,
They with their powers to Cawdebeck retire.

Like as a Hinde when shee her Calfe doth see,
Lighted by chance into a Lions pawes,
From which should shee aduenture it to free,
Shee must her selfe fill his deuouring lawes,
And yet her young one, still his prey must be,
(Shee so instructed is by Natures Lawes:)
With them so fares it, which must needs goe downe
If they would fight; and yet must loose the Towne:

Now doe they mount their Ordnance for the day,
Their scaling Ladders rearing to the walls,
Their battering Rammes against the gates they lay,
Their brazen slings send in the wilde-fire balls,
Baskets of twigs now carie stones and clay,
And to th'assault who furiously not falls;
The Spade and Pickax working are belowe,
Which then unfelt, yet gaue the greatest blowe.

Rampiers of earth the painefull Pyoners raise
With the walls equall, close upon the Dike,
To passe by which the Souldier that assayes,
On Planks thrust over, one him downe doth strike:
Him with a mall a second English payes,
A second French transpearc'd him with a Pyke:
That from the height of the embattel'd Towers,
Their mixed blood ranne downe the walls in showers.

A French man back into the Towne doth fall,
With a sheafe Arrow shot into the head;
An English man in scaling of the wall,
From the same place is by a stone struck dead;
Tumbling upon them logs of wood, and all,
That any way for their defence might sted:
The hills at hand re-ecchoing with the din
Of shouts without, and fearefull shrickes within.

When all at once the English men assaile,
The French within all valiantly defend,
And in a first assault, if any faile,
They by a second striue it to amend:
Out of the Towne come quarries thick as haile;
As thick againe their Shafts the English send:
The bellowing Canon from both sides doth rore,
With such a noyse as makes the Thunder pore.

Now upon one side you should heare a cry,
And all that Quarter clowded with a smother;
The like from that against it by and by;
As though the one were eccho to the other,
The King and Clarence so their turnes can ply:
And valiant Gloster showes himselfe their brother;
Whose Mynes to the besieg'd more mischiefe doe,
Then with th'assaults aboue, the other two.

An olde man sitting by the fier side,
Decrepit with extreamity of Age,
Stilling his little Grand-childe when it cride,
Almost distracted with the Batteries rage:
Sometimes doth speake it faire, sometimes doth chide,
As thus he seekes its mourning to asswage,
By chance a Bullet doth the chimney hit,
Which falling in, doth kill both him and it.

Whilst the sad weeping Mother sits her downe,
To give her little new-borne Babe the Pap:
A lucklesse quarry leveld at the Towne,
Kills the sweet Baby sleeping in her lap,
That with the fright shee falls into a swoone,
From which awak'd, and mad with the mishap;
As up a Rampire shreeking she doth clim,
Comes a great Shot, and strikes her lim from lim.

Whilst a sort runne confusedly to quench,
Some Pallace burning, or some fired Street,
Call'd from where they were fighting in the Trench;
They in their way with Balls of Wilde-fire meet,
So plagued are the miserable French,
Not aboue head, but also under feet:
For the fierce English vowe the Towne to take,
Or of it soone a heape of stones to make.

Hot is the Siege the English comming on,
As men so long to be kept out that scorne,
Carelesse of wounds as they were made of stone;
As with their teeth the walls they would have torne:
Into a Breach who quickly is not gone;
Is by the next behind him over-borne:
So that they found a place that gaue them way,
They neuer car'd what danger therein lay.

From ev'ry Quarter they their course must plye,
As't pleas'd the King them to th'assault to call:
Now on the Duke of Yorke the charge doth lye:

To Kent and Cornwall then the turne doth fall:
Then Huntingdon up to the walls they crye:
Then Suffolke, and then Excester; which all
In their meane Souldiers habits us'd to goe,
Taking such part as those that own'd them doe.

The men of Harflew rough excursions make,
Upon the English watchfull in their Tent,
Whose courages they to their cost awake,
With many a wound that often back them sent,
So proud a Sally that durst undertake,
And in the Chase pell mell amongst them went,
For on the way such ground of them they win,
That some French are shut out, some English in.

Nor idely sit our Men at Armes the while,
Foure thousand Horse that ev'ry day goe out;
And of the Field are Masters many a mile,
By putting the Rebellious French to rout;
No Peasants them with promises beguile:
Another bus'nesse they were come about;
For him they take, his Ransome must redeeme,
Onely French Crownes, the English men esteeme.

Whilst English Henry lastly meanes to trye:
By three vast Mynes, the walls to overthrowe.
The French men their approches that espye,
By Countermynes doe meete with them belowe,
And as opposed in the Workes they lye:
Up the Besieged the Besiegers blowe,
That stifled quite, with powder as with dust,
Longer to walls they found it vaine to trust.

Till Gaucourt then, and Tuttivile that were
The Townes Commanders, (with much perill) finde
The Resolution that the English beare;
As how their owne to yeelding were enclinde,
Summon to parly, off'ring frankly there;
If that ayde came not by a day assignde,
To give the Towne up, might their lives stand free:
As for their goods, at Henries will to be.

And having wonne their conduct to the King,
Those hardy Chiefes on whom the charge had layne:
Thither those well-fed Burgesses doe bring,
What they had off'red strongly to maintaine
In such a case, although a dang'rous thing,
Yet they so long upon their knees remaine:

That fiue dayes respight from his Grant they have,
Which was the most, they (for their lives) durst craue.

The time perfixed comming to expire,
And their reliefe ingloriously delay'd:
Nothing within their sight but sword, and fire;
And bloody Ensignes ev'ry where display'd:
The English still within themselves entire,
When all these things they seriously had way'd,
To Henries mercy found that they must trust,
For they perceiu'd their owne to be iniust.

The Ports are opened, weapons layd aside,
And from the walls th'Artillary displac'd:
The Armes of England are aduanc'd in pride:
The watch Tower, with Saint Georges Banner grac'd:
Live Englands Henry, all the people cride:
Into the Streetes their women runne in hast,
Bearing their little Children, for whose sake
They hop'd the King would the more mercy take.

The gates thus widened with the breath of Warre;
Their ample entrance to the English gaue:
There was no dore that then had any barre;
For of their owne not any thing they have:
When Henry comes on his Emperiall Carre:
To whom they kneele their lives alone to saue.
Strucken with wonder, when that face they sawe,
Wherein such mercy was, with so much awe.

And first themselves the English to secure,
Doubting what danger might be yet within;
The strongest Forts, and Citadell make sure,
To showe that they could keepe as well as win,
And though the spoyles them wondrously alure,
To fall to pillage e'r they will begin,
They shut each passage, by which any power
Might be brought on to hinder, but an hower.

That Conquering King which entring at the gate,
Borne by the presse as in the ayre he swamme:
Upon the suddaine layes aside his state,
And of a Lyon is become a Lambe:
He is not now what he was but of late:
But on his bare feete to the Church he came:
By his example, as did all the presse,
To give God thankes, for his first good successe.

And sends his Herauld to King Charles to say,
That though he thus was setled on his shore,
Yet he his Armes was ready downe to lay,
His ancient right if so he would restore:
But if the same he wilfully deny,
To stop th'effusion of their Subiects gore;
He frankly off'reth in a single fight,
With the young Daulphine to decide his right.

Eight dayes at Harflew he doth stay to heare,
What answere back, his Herauld him would bring:
But when he found that he was ne'r the neere;
And that the Daulphine meaneth no such thing,
As to fight single; nor that any were
To deale for composition from the King:
He casts for Callice to make forth his way,
And takes such Townes, as in his Iourneyes lay.

But first his bus'nesse he doth so contriue,
To curbe the Townes-men, should they chance to stirre
Of Armes, and Office he doth them depriue,
And to their roomes the English doth preferre:
Out of the Ports all Vagrants he doth driue,
And therein sets his Unckle Excester:
This done, to martch he bids the thundring Drummes,
To scourge proud France whẽ now her Cõqueror comes.

The King and Daulphine having understood,
How on his way this haughty Henry was
Over the Soame, which is a dangerous flood;
Pluckt downe the Bridges that might give him passe;
And ev'ry thing, if fit for humane food,
Caus'd to be forrag'd; (to a wondrous masse)
And more then this, his Iourneyes to fore-slowe,
He scarce one day unskirmish'd with, doth goe.

But on his march, in midst of all his foes;
He like a Lyon keepes them all at bay,
And when they seeme him strictly to enclose;
Yet through the thick'st he hewes him out a way:
Nor the proud Daulphine dare him to oppose;
Though off'ring oft his Army to fore-lay:
Nor all the power the enuious French can make,
Force him one foote, his path (but) to forsake.

And each day as his Army doth remove,
Marching along upon Soames Marshy side,
His men at Armes on their tall Horses prove,

To finde some shallow, over where to ryde,
But all in vaine against the Streame they stroue,
Till by the helpe of a laborious guide,
A Ford was found to set his Army ore
Which neuer had discovered beene before.

The newes divulg'd that he had waded Soame,
And safe to shore his Caridges had brought,
Into the Daulphins bosome strooke so home,
And one the weakenesse of King Charles so wrought;
That like the troubled Sea, when it doth Foame,
As in a rage, to beate the Rocks to nought;
So doe they storme, and curse on curse they heapt
Gainst those which should the passages have kept.

And at that time, both resident in Roan,
Thither for this assembling all the Peeres,
Whose Counsailes now must underprop their Throne
Against the Foe; which, not a man but feares;
Yet in a moment confident are growne,
When with fresh hopes, each one his fellow cheeres,
That ere the English to their Callis got,
Some for this spoile should pay a bloudy shot.

Therfore they both in solemne Counsaile satt,
With Berry and with Britaine their Alies;
Now speake they of this course, and then of that,
As to insnare him how they might diuise;
Something they faine would doe, but know not what,
At length the Duke Alanzon up doth rise,
And crauing silence of the King and Lords,
Against the English, brake into these words.

Had this unbridled youth an Army led,
That any way were worthy of your feare,
Against our Nation, that durst turne the head,
Such as the former English forces were,
This care of yours, your Countrey then might sted,
To tell you then, who longer can forbeare,
That into question, you our valour bring,
To call a Counsaile for so poore a thing.

A Route of tatter'd Rascalls starued so,
As forced through extreamity of need
To rake for scraps on Dunghils as they goe,
And on the Berries of the Shrubs to feed,
Besides with fluxes are enfeebled so,
And other foule diseases that they breed,

That they, there Armes disabled are to sway,
But in their march doe leaue them on the way.

And to our people but a handfull are,
Scarse thirtie thousand, when to Land they came,
Of which to England dayly some repayre,
Many from Harflew carried sicke and lame,
Fitter for Spittles, and the Surgions care,
Then with their Swords on us to winne them fame,
Unshod, and without stockings are the best,
And those by Winter miserably opprest.

To let them dye upon their march abroad,
And Fowles upon their Carkases to feed,
The heapes of them upon the common road
A great infection likely were to breed,
For our owne safeties see them then bestow'd,
And doe for them this charitable deede:
Under our Swords together let them fall,
And one that day they dye, be buried all.

This bold invectiue forc'd against the Foe,
Although it most of the Assembly seas'd,
Yet those which better did the English know,
Were but a little with his speeches pleas'd,
And that the Duke of Berry meant to showe:
Which when the murmure somewhat was appeas'd,
After a while their listning silence breakes,
And thus in answere of Alanzon speakes.

My Liedge, quoth he, and you my Lords, and Peeres,
Whom this great businesse chiefely doth concerne,
By my experience, now so many yeeres
To know the English I am not to learne;
Nor I more feeling have of humane feares
Than fitteth Manhood, nor doe hope to earne
Suffrage from any; but by zeale am wonne,
To speake my minde here, as the Duke hath done.

Th'euents of Warre are various (as I know)
And say, the losse upon the English light,
Yet may a dying man give such a blow,
As much may hinder his proud Conquerours might;
It is enough our puissant power to showe
To the weake English, now upon their flight,
When want, and winter, strongly spurre them on,
You else but slay them, that would faine be gon.

I like our Forces their first course should hold,
To skirmish with them, upon every stay,
But fight by no meanes with them, though they would,
Except they finde them forraging for pray,
So still you have them shut up in a Fould,
And still to Callis keepe them in their way;
So Fabius wearied Hanibal, so we
May English Henry, pleased if you be.

And of the English rid your Countrey cleane,
If on their backs, but Callice walles they win,
Whose Frontier Townes you easly may maintaine,
With a strong Army still to keepe them in;
Then let our Ships make good the mouth of Seyne,
And at your pleasure Harflew you may winne,
Ere with Supplys againe they can inuade,
Spent in the Voyage lately hither made.

That day at Poyteers, in that bloudy Field,
The sudaine turne in that great Battell then,
Shall euer teach me, whilest I Armes can weeld,
Neuer to trust to multitudes of men;
Twas the first day that ere I wore a Sheeld,
Oh let me neuer see the like agen!
Where their Blacke Edward such a Battell wonne
As to behold it might amaze the Sunne.

There did I see our conquered Fathers fall,
Before the English on that fatall ground,
When as to ours their number was but small,
And with brave Spirits France ne'r did more abound,
Yet oft that Battaile into minde I call,
Whereas of ours, one man seemd all one wound,
I instance this; yet humbly here submit
My selfe to fight, if you shall thinke it fit.

The Marshall and the Constable about
To second, what this sager Duke had said:
The youthfull Lords into a cry brake out,
Gainst their opinions, so that over-sway'd,
Some seeming of their Loyalties to doubt;
Alanzon as an Oracle obay'd,
And not a French then present, but doth sweare
To kill an English if ynow there were.

A Herault posted presently away,
The King of England to the field to dare,
To bid him cease his spoyle, nor to delay

Gainst the French power his forces but prepare:
For that King Charles determin'd to display
His bloody Ensignes, and through France declare
The day, and place, that Henry should set downe,
In which their Battailes, should dispose the Crowne.

This newes to Henry by the Herault brought,
As one dispassion'd soberly (quoth he)
Had your King pleas'd, we sooner might have fought;
For now my Souldiers much enfeebled be:
Nor day, nor place, for Battaile shall be sought
By English Henry: but if he seeke me,
I to my vtmost will my selfe defend,
And to th'Almighties pleasure leaue the end.

The brute of this intended Battaile spred,
The coldnesse of each sleeping courage warmes,
And in the French that daring boldnesse bred:
Like casting Bees that they arise in swarmes,
Thinking the English downe so farre to tred,
As past that day ne'r more to rise in Armes,
T'extirpe the name, if possible it were,
At least not after to be heard of there.

As when you see the enuious Crowe espye,
Something that shee doth naturally detest:
With open throat how shee doth squall and crye;
And from the next Groue calleth in the rest,
And they for those beyond them bawling flye,
Till their foule noyse doth all the ayre infest:
Thus French, the French to this great Battaile call,
Upon their swords to see the English fall.

And to the King when seriously one tolde,
With what an Host he should encountred be,
Gam noting well, the King did him behold,
In the reporting; Merrily (quoth he)
My Liege I'le tell you if I may be bold,
We will diuide this Army into three:
One part we'll kill, the second prisoners stay;
And for the third, we'll leaue to runne away.

But for the Foe came hourely in so fast,
Lest they his Army should disordred take:
The King who wisely doth the worst forecast,
His speedy martch doth presently forsake,
Into such forme and his Battalion cast;
That doe their worst they should not eas'ly shake:

For that his scouts which forrag'd had the Coast,
Bad him at hand expect a puissant Host.

On which ere long the English Vanward light,
Which York, of men the bravest, doth command,
When either of them in the others sight,
He caus'd the Army instantly to stand,
As though preparing for a present Fight,
And rideth forth from his couragious Band,
To view the French, whose numbers over spread,
The troubled Country on whose earth they tread.

Now were both Armies got upon that ground,
As on a Stage, where they their strengthes must trye,
Whence from the wydth of many a gaping wound,
There's many a soule into the Ayre must flye:
Meane while the English that some ease had found;
By the aduantage of a Village nie,
There set them downe the Battell to abide,
Where they the place had strongly fortifide.

Made drunke with pride the haughty French disdaine,
Lesse then their owne, a multitude to view,
Nor aske of God the victory to gaine,
Upon the English wext so poore and fewe,
To stay their slaughter thinking it a paine,
And lastly to that insolence they grewe,
Quoyts, Lots, and Dice for Englishmen to cast,
And sweare to pay, the Battaile being past.

For knots of corde to ev'ry Towne they send,
The Captiu'd English that they caught to binde,
For to perpetuall slau'ry they intend:
Those that alive they on the Field should finde,
So much as that they fear'd lest they should spend
Too many English, wherefore they assignde
Some to keepe fast those, fayne that would be gon
After the Fight, to try their Armes upon.

One his bright sharpe-eg'd Semiter doth showe,
Off'ring to lay a thousand Crownes (in pride)
That he two naked English at one blowe,
Bound back to back will at the wasts diuide,
Some bett his sword will do't, some others no,
After the Battaile, and they'll have it tride:
Another wafts his Blade about his head,
And shewes them how their hamstrings he will shread.

They part their prisoners, passing them for debt,
And in their Ransome ratibly accord
To a Prince of ours, a Page of theirs they set;
And a French Lacky to an English Lord;
As for our Gentry them to hyre they'll let,
And as good cheape as they can them afford,
Branded for Slaues that if they hapt to stray,
Knowne by the marke, them any one might slay.

And cast to make a Chariot for the King,
Painted with Antickes, and ridiculous toyes,
In which they meane to Paris him to bring,
To make sport to their Madames and their Boyes,
And will have Rascalls, Rymes of him to sing,
Made in his mock'ry; and in all these joyes,
They bid the Bells to ring, and people crie,
Before the Battaile, France and Victorie.

And to the King and Daulphine sent away
(Who at that time residing were in Roane)
To be partakers of that glorious day:
Wherein the English should be overthrowne,
Lest that of them ensuing times should say,
That for their safety they forsooke their owne:
When France did that brave victory obtaine,
That shall her lasting'st monument remaine.

The poore distressed Englishmen the whiles,
Not dar'd by doubt, and lesse appaul'd with dread
Of their Arm'd Pykes, some sharpning are the pyles,
The Archer grinding his barb'd Arrow head:
Their Bills and Blades, some whetting are with Files:
And some their Armours strongly Riueted:
Some pointing Stakes to stick into the ground,
To guard the Bow-men, and their Horse to wound.

The night fore-running this most dreadfull day:
The French that all to iollity encline:
Some fall to dancing, some againe to play:
And some are drinking to this great Designe:
But all in pleasure spend the night away:
The Tents with lights, the Fields with Boone-fires shine:
The common Souldiers Free-mens Catches sing:
With showtes and laughter all the Campe doth ring.

The wearied English watchfull o'r their Foes,
(The depth of night then drawing on so fast)
That fayne a little would themselves repose,

With thanks to God, doe take that small repast
Which that poore Village willingly bestowes:
And having plac'd their Sentinels at last,
They fall to Prayer, and in their Cabins blest,
T'refresh their spirits, then tooke them to their rest.

In his Pavillion Princely Henry lay'd,
Whilst all his Army round about him slept,
His restlesse head upon his Helmet stay'd,
For carefull thoughts his eyes long waking kept:
Great God (quoth he) withdraw not now thy ayde:
Nor let my Father Henries sinnes be heapt
On my transgressions, up the Summe to make,
For which thou may'st me vtterly forsake.

King Richards wrongs, to minde, Lord doe not call,
Nor how for him my Father did offend,
From us alone deriue not thou his fall,
Whose odious life caus'd his untimely end,
That by our Almes be expiated all:
Let not that sinne on me his Sonne desend,
When as his body I translated have,
And buried in an honourable Graue.

These things thus pondring, sorrow-ceasing sleepe,
From cares to rescue his much troubled minde,
Upon his Eye-lids stealingly doth creepe,
And in soft slumbers every sense doth binde,
(As undisturbed every one to keepe)
When as that Angell to whom God assign'd,
The guiding of the English, gliding downe
The silent Campe doth with fresh courage crowne.

His glittering wings he gloriously displaies,
Over the Hoste as every way it lyes
With golden Dreames their trauell, and repaies,
This Herault from the Rector of the skies,
In Vision warnes them not to use delayes,
But to the Battell cheerefully to rise,
And be victorious, for that day at hand,
He would amongst them for the English stand.

The dawne scarse drewe the curtaines of the East,
But the late wearied Englishmen awake,
And much refreshed with a little rest
Themselves soone ready for the Battaile make,
Not any one but feeleth in his breast,
That sprightly fire which Courage bids him take,

For ere the Sunne next rising went to bed,
The French by them in triumph should be led.

And from their Cabins, ere the French arose,
(Drown'd in the pleasure of the passed night,)
The English cast their Battailes to dispose,
Fit for the ground whereon they were to fight:
Foorth that brave King couragious Henry goes,
An hower before that it was fully light,
To see if there might any place be found,
To give his Hoste aduantage by the ground.

Where twas his hap a Quicksett hedge to view,
Well growne in height; and for his purpose thin,
Yet by the Ditch upon whose banke it grew,
He found it to be difficult to winne,
Especially if those of his were true,
Amongst the shrubbs that he should set within,
By which he knew their strength of Horse must come,
If they would euer charge his Vanguard home.

And of three hundred Archers maketh choice,
Some to be taken out of every Band,
The strongest Bowmen, by the generall voyce,
Such as beside were valient of their hand,
And to be so imployed, as would rejoyce,
Appointing them behinde the hedge to stand,
To shrowde themselves from sight, and to be mute,
Untill a signall freely bad them shute.

The gamesome Larke now got upon her Wing,
As twere the English earely to awake,
And to wide Heaven her cheerefull notes doth sing,
As shee for them would intercession make,
Nor all the noyse that from below doth spring,
Her ayrie walke can force her to forsake,
Of some much noted, and of others lesse,
But yet of all presaging good successe.

The lazie French their leisure seem to take,
And in their Cabins keepe themselves so long,
Till flocks of Rauens them with noyse awake,
Over the Army like a Cloud that hong,
Which greater haste inforceth them to make,
When with their croaking all the Countrey rong,
Which boaded slaughter as the most doe say,
But by the French it turned was this way.

That this diuyning Foule well understood,
Upon that place much gore was to be spill'd,
And as those Birds doe much delight in blood,
With humane flesh would have their gorges fill'd,
So waited they upon their Swords for food,
To feast upon the English being kill'd,
Then little thinking that these came in deed
On their owne mangled Carkases to feed.

When soone the French preparing for the Field,
Their armed troops are setting in array,
Whose wondrous numbers they can hardly weeld,
The place too little whereupon they lay,
They therefore to necessitie must yeeld,
And into Order put them as they may,
Whose motion sounded like to Nilus fall,
That the vaste ayre was deafned therewithall.

The Constable, and Admirall of France,
With the grand Marshall, men of great command:
The Dukes of Burbon, and of Orleance,
Some for their place, some for their birth-right stand,
The Daulphine of Averney (to aduance
His worth and honour) of a puissant hand:
The Earle of Ewe in Warre that had beene bred,
These mighty men the mighty Vanward led.

The mayne brought forward by the Duke of Barre,
Neuers, and Beamont, men of speciall name:
Alanzon thought, not equall'd in this Warre,
With them Salines, Rous, and Grandpre came,
Their long experience, who had fetcht from farre,
Whom this expected Conquest doth enflame,
Consisting most of Crosbowes, and so great,
As France her selfe it well might seeme to threat.

The Duke of Brabant of high valour knowne,
The Earles of Marle, and Faconbridge the Reare,
To Arthur Earle of Richmount's selfe alone,
They leaue the Right wing to be guided there:
Lewes of Burbon, second yet to none,
Led on the left; with him that mighty Peere
The Earle of Vandome, who of all her men
Large France entytled, her great Master then.

The Duke of Yorke the English Vanward guides,
Of our strong Archers, that consisted most;
Which with our Horse was wing'd on both the sides:

T'affront so great and terrible an Host;
There valiant Fanhope, and there Beamount rides,
With Willoughby which scowred had the Coast,
That morning early, and had seene at large,
How the Foe came, that then they were to charge.

Henry himselfe, on the mayne Battell brings,
Nor can these Legions of the French affright
This Mars of men, this King of earthly Kings:
Who seem'd to be much pleased with the sight,
As one ordayn'd t'accomplish mighty things;
Who to the Field came in such brau'ry dight:
As to the English boades succesfull luck
Before one stroke, on either side was struck.

In Warlike state the Royall Standard borne
Before him, as in splendrous Armes he road,
Whilst his coruetting Courser seem'd in scorne
To touch the earth whereon he proudly troad,
Lillyes, and Lyons quarterly adorne;
His Shield, and his Caparison doe load:
Upon his Helme a Crowne with Diamonds deckt,
Which through the Field their Radient fiers reflect.

The Duke of Gloster neere to him agen,
T'assist his Brother in that dreadfull day,
Oxford and Suffolke both true Marshiall men,
Ready to keepe the Battell in Array,
To Excester there was appointed then
The Reare; on which their second succours lay:
Which were the youth, most of the Noblest blood,
Under the Ensignes of their names that stood.

Then of the stakes he doth the care commend,
To certaine troupes that actiue were and strong,
Onely diuis'd the Archers to defend,
Pointed with Iron and of fiue foote long;
To be remov'd still which way they should bend,
Where the French Horse should thick'st upon them throng
Which when the Host to charge each other went,
Show'd his great wit that first did them inuent.

Both Armies sit, and at the point to fight,
The French themselves assuring of the day;
Send to the King of England (as in spight)
To know what he would for his Ransome pay,
Who with this answere doth their scorne requite:
I pray thee Herault wish the French to stay,

And e'r the day be past, I hope to see,
That for their Ransomes they shall send to me.

The French which found how little Henry makes,
Of their vaine boasts, as set therewith on fire,
Whilst each one to his Ensigne him betakes;
The Constable to raise their spleene the hyer,
Thus speakes: Brave friends now for your Grandsires sakes,
Your Country, Honours, or what may inspire
Your soules with courage, straine up all your powers,
To make this day victoriously ours.

Forward stout French, your valours and aduance,
By taking vengeance for our Fathers slaine,
And strongly fixe the Diadem of France,
Which to this day unsteady doth remaine:
Now with your swords their Traytours bosomes lance,
And with their bloods wash out that ancient staine,
And make our earth drunke with the English gore,
Which hath of ours oft surfited before.

Let not one live in England once to tell,
What of their King, or of the rest became:
Nor to the English, what in France befell:
But what is bruted by the generall fame:
But now the Drummes began so lowd to yell,
As cut off further what he would declame:
And Henry seeing them on so fast to make,
Thus to his Souldiers comfortably spake.

Thinke but upon the iustnesse of our cause,
And he's no man their number that will wey;
Thus our great Grandsire purchas'd his applause,
The more they are, the greater is our prey,
We'll hand in hand wade into dangers iawes,
And let report to England this Conuey
That it for me no Ransome e'r shall rayse,
Either I'le Conquer, or here end my dayes.

It were no glory for us to subdue
Them, then our number, were the French no more;
When in one Battaile twice our Fathers slue,
Three times so many as themselves before,
But to doe something that were strange and new:
Wherefore (I aske you) Came we to this shore;
Upon these French our Fathers wan renowne,
And with their swords we'll hewe yan Forrest downe.

The meanest Souldier if in Fight he take,
The greatest Prince in yonder Army knowne,
Without controule shall him his prisoner make,
And have his Ransome freely as his owne:
Now English lyes our Honour at the stake,
And now or neuer be our Valour showne:
God and our Cause, Saint George for England stands,
Now Charge them English, fortune guide your hands.

When hearing one wish all the valiant men
At home in England, with them present were;
The King makes answere instantly agen,
I would not have one man more then is here:
If we subdue, lesse should our praise be then:
If overcome, lesse losse shall England beare:
And to our numbers we should give that deede,
Which must from Gods owne powerfull hand proceede.

The dreadfull Charge the Drummes & Trumpets sound,
With hearts exalted, though with humbled eyes,
When as the English kneeling on the ground,
Extend their hands up to the glorious skyes;
Then from the earth as though they did rebound,
Actiue as fire immediatly they rise:
And such a shrill showt from their throats they sent,
As made the French to stagger as they went.

Wherewith they stopt, when Erpingham which led
The Armie, sawe, the showt had made them stand,
Wafting his Warder thrice about his head,
He cast it up with his auspicious hand,
Which was the signall through the English spread,
That they should Charge: which as a dread command
Made them rush on, yet with a second rore,
Frighting the French worse then they did before.

But when they sawe the Enemie so slowe,
Which they expected faster to come on,
Some scattering Shot they sent out as to showe,
That their approach they onely stood upon;
Which with more feruour made their rage to glowe,
So much disgrace that they had under-gone.
Which to amend with Ensignes let at large,
Upon the English furiously they Charge.

At the full Moone looke how th'unweldy Tide,
Shou'd by some Tempest that from Sea doth rise
At the full height, against the ragged side

Of so me rough Cliffe (of a Gigantick sise)
Foming with rage impetuously doth ride;
The angry French (in no lesse furious wise)
Of men at Armes upon their ready Horse,
Assayle the English to dispierce their force.

When as those Archers there in Ambush layde,
Having their Broad side as they came along,
With their barb'd Arrowes the French Horses payde:
And in their flankes like cruell Hornets stong:
They kick and crie, of late that proudly nayde:
And from their seats their Armed Riders flong:
They ranne together flying from the Dike,
And make their Riders one another strike.

And whilst the Front of the French Vanguard makes,
Upon the English thinking them to Route,
Their Horses runne upon the Armed stakes,
And being wounded, turne themselves about:
The Bit into his teeth the Courser takes,
And from his Rank flyes with his Master out,
Who either hurts or is hurt of his owne,
If in the throng not both together throwne.

Tumbling on heapes, some of their Horses cast
With their foure feete all up into the ayre:
Under whose backs their Masters breath their last:
Some breake their Raynes, and thence their Riders beare:
Some with their feete stick in the Stirups fast,
By their fierce lades, are trayled here and there:
Entangled in their Bridles, one back drawes,
And pluckes the Bit out of anothers jawes.

With showers of Shafts yet still the English ply
The French so fast, upon the point of flight:
With the mayne Battell yet stood Henry by,
Not all this while had medled in the Fight,
Upon the Horses as in Chase they flye,
Arrowes so thick, in such aboundance light,
That their broad buttocks men like Butts might see,
Whereat for pastime Bow-men shooting be.

When soone De Linnies and Sureres hast,
To ayde their friends put to this shamefull foyle,
With two light wings of Horse which had beene plac't,
Still to supply where any should recoyle:
But yet their Forces they but vainely waste,
For being light, into the generall spoyle.

Great losse De Linnies shortly doth sustaine,
Yet scapes himselfe; but brave Sureres slaine.

The King who sees how well his Vanguard sped,
Sends his command that instantly it stay,
Desiring Yorke so bravely that had led,
To hold his Souldiers in their first array,
For it the Conflict very much might sted,
Somewhat to fall aside, and give him way,
Till full up to him he might bring his power,
And make the Conquest compleate in an hower.

Which Yorke obayes, and up King Henry comes,
When for his guidance he had got him roome.
The dreadfull bellowing of whose strait-brac'd Drummes,
To the French sounded like the dreadfull doome,
And them with such stupidity benummes,
As though the earth had groaned from her wombe,
For the grand slaughter ne'r began till then,
Covering the earth with multitudes of men.

Upon the French what Englishman not falls,
(By the strong Bowmen beaten from their Steeds)
With Battle-axes, Halberts, Bills, and Maules,
Where, in the slaughter every one exceedes,
Where every man, his fellow forward calls,
And shows him where some great-born Frenchman bleeds
Whilst Scalps about like broken pot sherds fly,
And kill, kill, kill, the Conquering English cry.

Now wexed horror to the very height,
And scarse a man but wet-shod went in gore,
As two together are in deadly fight,
And to death wounded, as one tumbleth ore,
This Frenchman falling, with his very weight
Doth kill another strucken downe before,
As he againe so falling, likewise feeles
His last breath hastned by anothers heeles.

And whilst the English eagerly pursue
The fearefull French before them still that fly,
The points of Bills and Halbers they imbrue
In their sicke Bowels, beaten downe that lye,
No man respects how, or what blood he drew,
Nor can heare those that for their mercie cry.
Ears are damm'd up with howles and hellish sounds
One fearefull noyse a fearefuller confounds.

When the couragious Constable of France,
Th'unlucky Vanguard valiantly that led,
Sawe the day turn'd by this disastrous chance,
And how the French before the English fled;
O stay (quoth he) your Ensignes yet aduance,
Once more upon the Enemy make head:
Neuer let France say, we were vanquisht so,
With our backs basely turn'd upon our Foe.

Whom the Chattillyon hapned to accost,
And seeing thus the Constable dismayde:
Shift noble Lord (quoth he) the day is lost,
If the whole world upon the match were layde,
I cannot thinke but that Black Edwards Ghost
Assists the English, and our Horse hath frayde;
If not, some Diuels they have with them then,
That fight against us in the shapes of men.

Not I my Lord, the Constable replies:
By my blest soule, the Field I will not quit:
Whilst two brave Battailes are to bring supplies:
Neither of which one stroke have strucken yet:
Nay (quoth Dampeir) I doe not this aduise
More then your selfe, that I doe feare a whit:
Spurre up my Lord, then side to side with mee,
And that I feare not, you shall quickly see.

They struck their Rowells to the bleeding sides
Of their fierce Steeds into the ayre that sprong:
And as their fury at that instant guides:
They thrust themselves into the murth'ring throng,
Where such bad fortune those brave Lords betides:
The Admirall from off his Horse was flong,
For the sterne English downe before them beere
All that withstand, the Pesant and the Peere.

Which when the noble Constable with griefe,
Doth this great Lord upon the ground behold;
In his account so absolute a Chiefe,
Whose death through France he knew would be condol'd,
Like a brave Knight to yeeld his friend reliefe,
Doing as much as possibly he could,
Both horse and man is borne into the mayne,
And from his friend not halfe a furlong slayne.

Now Willoughby upon his well-Arm'd Horse,
Into the midst of this Battalion brought,
And valiant Fanhope no whit lesse in force,

Himselfe hath thither through the squadrons raught,
Whereas the English without all remorce,
(Looking like men that deepely were distraught)
Smoking with sweat, besmear'd with dust and blood,
Cut into Cantels all that them withstood.

Yet whilst thus hotely they hold up the Chase
Upon the French, and had so high a hand:
The Duke of Burbon to make good his place,
Inforc'd his troupes (with much adoe) to stand,
To whom the Earle of Suffolke makes a pace,
Bringing a fresh, and yet-unfought-with Band:
Of valiant Bill-men, Oxford with successe,
Up with his Troupes doth with the other presse.

When in comes Orleance, quite thrust off before,
By those rude crowdes that from the English ran,
Encouraging stout Burbons Troupes the more,
T'affront the Foe that instantly began:
Faine would the Duke (if possible) restore,
(Doing as much as could be done by man)
Their Honour lost, by this their late Defeate,
And caused onely, by their base Retreate.

Their men at Armes their Lances closely lock
One in another, and come up so round,
That by the strength and horrour of the shock,
They forc'd the English to forsake their ground,
Shrinking no more then they had beene a Rock,
Though by the Shafts receiuing many a wound,
As they would showe, that they were none of those,
That turn'd their backs so basely to their Foes.

Panting for breath, his Murrian in his hand,
Woodhouse comes in as back the English beare,
My Lords (quoth he) what now inforc'd to stand,
When smiling Fortune off'reth us so faire,
The French lye yonder like to wreakes of sand,
And you by this our glory but impaire:
Or now, or neuer, your first Fight maintaine,
Chatillyon and the Constable are slaine.

Hand over head pell mell upon them ronne,
If you will prove the Masters of the day,
Ferrers and Greystock have so bravely done,
That I enuie their glory, and dare say,
From all the English, they the Gole have woone;
Either let's share, or they'll beare all away.

This spoke, his Ax about his head he flings,
And hasts away, as though his heeles had winges.

The Incitation of this youthfull Knight,
Besides amends for their Retrayte to make,
Doth re-enforce their courage, with their might:
A second Charge with speed to undertake;
Neuer before were they so mad to fight,
When valiant Fanhope thus the Lords bespake,
Suffolke and Oxford as braue Earles you be,
Once more beare up with Willoughby and me.

Why now, me think'st I heare braue Fanhope speake,
Quoth noble Oxford, thou hast thy desire:
These words of thine shall yan Battalion breake:
And for my selfe I neuer will retire,
Untill our Teene upon the French we wreake:
Or in this our last enterprise expire:
This spoke, their Gauntlets each doth other giue,
And to the Charge as fast as they could driue.

That slaughter seem'd to haue but stay'd for breath,
To make the horrour to ensue the more:
With hands besmear'd with blood, when meager Death
Looketh more grisly then he did before:
So that each body seem'd but as a sheath
To put their swords in, to the Hilts in gore:
As though that instant were the end of all,
To fell the French, or by the French to fall.

Looke how you see a field of standing Corne,
When some strong winde in Summer haps to blowe,
At the full height, and ready to be shorne,
Rising in waues, how it doth come and goe
Forward and backward, so the crowds are borne,
Or as the Edie turneth in the flowe:
And aboue all the Bills and Axes play,
As doe the Attoms in the Sunny ray.

Now with mayne blowes their Armours are unbras'd,
And as the French before the English fled,
With their browne Bills their recreant backs they baste,
And from their shoulders their faint Armes doe shred,
One with a gleaue neere cut off by the waste,
Another runnes to ground with halfe a head:
Another stumbling falleth in his flight,
Wanting a legge, and on his face doth light.

The Dukes who found their force thus overthrowne,
And those fewe left them ready still to route,
Having great skill, and no lesse courage showne;
Yet of their safeties much began to doubt,
For having fewe about them of their owne,
And by the English so impal'd about,
Saw that to some one they themselves must yeeld,
Or else abide the fury of the field.

They put themselves on those victorious Lords,
Who led the Vanguard with so good successe,
Bespeaking them with honourable words,
Themselves their prisoners freely and confesse,
Who by the strength of their commanding swords,
Could hardly saue them from the slaught'ring presse,
By Suffolks ayde till they away were sent,
Who with a Guard conuay'd them to his Tent.

When as their Souldiers to eschew the sack,
Gainst their owne Battell bearing in their flight,
By their owne French are strongly beaten back:
Lest they their Ranks, should have disord'red quight,
So that those men at Armes goe all to wrack
Twixt their owne friends, and those with whom they fight,
Wherein disorder and destruction seem'd
To striue, which should the powerfullest be deem'd.

And whilst the Daulphine of Auerney cryes,
Stay men at Armes, let Fortune doe her worst,
And let that Villaine from the field that flyes
By Babes yet to be borne, be euer curst:
All under Heaven that we can hope for, lyes
On this dayes battell, let me be the first
That turn'd yee back upon your desperate Foes,
To saue our Honours, though our lyues we lose.

To whom comes in the Earle of Ewe, which long
Had in the Battaile ranged here and there,
A thousand Bills, a thousand Bowes among,
And had seene many spectakles of feare,
And finding yet the Daulphins spirit so strong,
By that which he had chanst from him to heare,
Upon the shoulder claps him, Prince quoth he,
Since I mast fall, ô let me fall with thee.

Scarse had he spoke, but th'English them inclose,
And like to Mastiues fircely on them flew,
Who with like Courage strongly them oppose,

When the Lord Beamont, who their Armings knewe,
Their present perill to brave Suffolke shewes,
Quoth hee, Lo where Dauerny are and Ewe,
In this small time, who since the Field begun,
Have done as much, as can by men be done.

Now slaughter cease me, if I doe not greeue,
Two so brave Spirits should be untimely slaine,
Lies there no way (my Lord) them to releeue,
And for their Ransomes two such to retaine:
Quoth Suffolke, come weele hazad their repreeue,
And share our Fortunes, in they goe amaine,
And with such danger through the presse they wade,
As of their lives but small account they made.

Yet ere they through the clustred Crouds could get,
Oft downe on those, trod there to death that lay,
The valient Daulphin had discharg'd his debt,
Then whom no man had bravelier seru'd that day.
The Earle of Ewe, and wondrous hard beset:
Had left all hope of life to scape away:
Till noble Beamont and brave Suffolke came,
And as their prisoner seas'd him by his name.

Now the mayne Battaile of the French came on,
The Vanward vanquisht, quite the Field doth flye,
And other helpes besides this, have they none:
But that their hopes doe on their mayne relye,
And therefore now it standeth them upon,
To fight it bravely, or else yeeld, or dye:
For the fierce English charge so home and sore,
As in their hands loues thunderbolts they bore.

The Duke of Yorke, who since the fight begun,
Still in the top of all his Troopes was seene,
And things wellneere beyond beleefe had done,
Which of his Fortune, made him overweene,
Himselfe so farre into the maine doth runne,
So that the French which quickly got betweene
Him and his succours, that great Chiefetaine slue,
Who bravely fought whilest any breath he drew.

The newes soone brought to this Couragious King,
Orespred his face with a distempred Fire,
Though making little shew of any thing,
Yet to the full his eyes exprest his Ire,
More then before the Frenchmen menacing;
And hee was heard thus softly to respire:

Well, of thy blood reuenged will I bee,
Or ere one houre be past Ile follow thee.

When as the frolike Caualry of France,
That in the head of the maine Battaile came,
Perceiu'd the King of England to aduance,
To Charge in person; It doth them inflame,
Each one well hoping it might be his chance
To sease upon him, which was all their ayme,
Then with the bravest of the English mett,
Themselves that there before the King had sett.

When the Earle of Cornewal with unusuall force,
Encounters Grandpre (next that came to hand)
In Strength his equall, blow for blow they scorce,
Weelding their Axes as they had beene wands,
Till the Earle tumbles Grandpre from his Horse
Over whom straight the Count Salines stands,
And lendeth Cornwal such a blow withall,
Over the Crupper that he makes him fall.

Cornwal recovers, for his Armes were good,
And to Salines maketh up againe,
Who changde such boysterous buffets, that the blood,
Doth through the Ioints of their strong Armour straine,
Till Count Salines sunck downe where he stood,
Blamount who sees the Count Salines slaine,
Straight copes with Cornwal beaten out of breath
Till Kent comes in, and rescues him from death.

Kent upon Blamount furiously doth flye,
Who at the Earle with no lesse courage struck,
And one the other with such knocks they plye,
That eithers Axe in th'others Helmet stuck;
Whilst they are wrastling, crossing thigh with thigh;
Their Axes pykes, which soonest out should pluck:
They, fall to ground like in their Casks to smother,
With their clutcht Gauntlets cuffing one another.

Couragious Cluet grieued at the sight
Of his friend Blamounts unexpected fall,
Makes in to lend him all the ayde he might;
Whose comming seem'd the stout Lord Scales to call,
Betwixt whom then began a mortall fight,
When instantly fell in Sir Phillip Hall,
Gainst him goes Roussy, in then Lovell ran,
Whom next Count Moruyle chuseth as his man.

Their Curates are unriuetted with blowes,
With horrid wounds their breasts and faces slasht;
There drops a cheeke, and there falls off a nose:
And in ones face his fellowes braines are dasht;
Yet still the Better with the English goes;
The earth of France with her owne blood is washt;
They fall so fast, she scarse affords them roome,
That one mans Trunke becomes anothers Toombe.

When Suffolk chargeth Huntingdon with sloth,
Over himselfe too wary to have bin,
And had neglected his fast plighted troth
Upon the Field, the Battaile to begin,
That where the one was, there they would be both;
When the stout Earle of Huntingdon, to win
Trust with his friends; doth this himselfe enlarge
To this great Earle who dares him thus to charge.

My Lord (quoth he) it is not that I feare,
More then your selfe, that so I have not gone;
But that I have beene forced to be neare
The King, whose person I attend upon,
And that I doubt not but to make appeare
Now, if occasion shall but call me on,
Looke round about my Lord, if you can see,
Some brave aduenture worthy you and me.

See yan proud Banner, of the Duke of Barres,
Me thinkst it wafts us, and I heare it say,
Wher's that couragious Englishman that darres,
Aduenture, but to carry me away,
This were a thing, now worthy of our warres;
I'st true, quoth Suffolke, by this blessed day,
On, and weele have it, sayst thou so indeed,
Quoth Huntingdon, then Fortune be our speed.

And through the Ranckes then rushing in their pride,
They make a Lane; about them so they lay,
Foote goes with foote, and side is joynde to side,
They strike downe all that stand within their way,
And to direct them, have no other guide,
But as they see the multitude to sway;
And as they passe, the French as to defie,
Saint George for England and the King they cry.

By their examples, each brave English blood,
Upon the Frenchmen for their Ensignes runne,
Thick there as trees within a well-growne wood:

Where great Atchiements instantly were done,
Against them toughly whilst that Nation stood,
But ô what man his destinie can shunne
That Noble Suffolke there is overthrowne,
When he much valour sundry wayes hath showne.

Which the proud English further doth provoke,
Who to destruction bodily were bent,
That the maine Battaile instantly they broke,
Upon the French so furiously they went
And not an English but doth scorne a stroake,
If to the ground it not a Frenchman sent,
Who weake with wounds, their weapons from them threw,
With which the English fearefully them slue.

Alanzon backe upon the Reareward borne,
By those unarm'd that from the English fled,
All further hopes then vtterly forlorne,
His Noble heart in his full Bosome bled;
What Fate, quoth he, our overthrowe hath sworne,
Must France a Prisoner be to England led,
Well, if she be so, yet Ile let her see,
She beares my Carkasse with her, and not me.

And puts his Horse upon his full Careere,
When with the courage of a valiant Knight
(As one that knew not, or forgot to feare)
He tow'rds King Henry maketh in the fight,
And all before him as he downe doth beare,
Upon the Duke of Glocester doth light:
Which on the youthfull Chiualry doth bring,
Scarse two Pykes length that came before the King.

Their Staues both strongly riuetted with steele,
At the first stroke each other they astound,
That as they staggering from each other reele;
The Duke of Gloster falleth to the ground:
When as Alanzon round about doth wheele,
Thinking to lend him his last deadly wound:
In comes the King his Brothers life to saue
And to this brave Duke, a fresh on-set gaue.

When as themselves like Thunderbolts they shot,
One at the other, and the Lightning brake
Out of their Helmets, and againe was not,
E'r of their strokes, the eare a sound could take
Betwixt them two, the Conflict grew so hot,
Which those about them so amaz'd doth make,

That they stood still as wondring at the sight,
And quite forgot that they themselves must fight.

Upon the King Alanzon prest so sore,
That with a stroke (as he was wondrous strong)
He cleft the Crowne that on his Helme he wore,
And tore his Plume that to his heeles it hong:
Then with a second brus'd his Helme before,
That it his forehead pittifully wroong:
As some that sawe it certainly had thought,
The King therewith had to the ground beene brought.

But Henry soone Alanzons Ire to quit,
(As now his valour lay upon the Rack)
Upon the face the Duke so strongly hit,
As in his Saddle layde him on his back,
And once perceiuing that he had him split,
Follow'd his blowes, redoubling thwack on thwack:
Till he had lost his Stirups, and his head
Hung where his Horse was like thereon to tread.

When soone two other seconding their Lord,
His kind Companions in this glorious prize,
Hoping againe the Duke to have restor'd,
If to his feet his Armes would let him rise:
On the Kings Helme their height of fury scor'd;
Who like a Dragon fiercely on them flies,
And on his body slew them both, whilst he
Recovering was their ayde againe to be.

The King thus made the Master of the Fight:
The Duke calls to him as he there doth lye:
Henry I'le pay my Ransome, doe me right:
I am the Duke Alanzon; it is I.
The King to saue him putting all his might,
Yet the rude Souldiers, with their showt and crie,
Quite drown'd his voyce, his Helmet being shut,
And, that brave Duke into small peeces cut.

Report once spred, through the distracted Host,
Of their prime hope, the Duke Alanzon slayne:
That flower of France, on whom they trusted most:
They found their valour was but then in vayne:
Like men their hearts that vtterly had lost,
Who slowly fled before, now ranne amayne.
Nor could a man be found, but that dispaires
Seeing the Fate both of themselves and theirs.

The Duke Neuers, now in this sad retreat,
By Dauid Gam and Morisby persude,
(Who throughly chaf'd, neere melted into sweat,
And with French blood their Poleaxes imbrud)
They sease upon him following the defeate,
Amongst the faint, and fearefull multitude;
When a contention fell betweene them twaine,
To whom the Duke should rightfully pertaine.

I must confesse thou hadst him first in chase,
Quoth Morrisby; but lefts him in the throng,
Then put I on; quoth Gam, hast thou the face,
Insulting Knight, to offer me this wrong;
Quoth Morrisby, who shall decide the case,
Let him confesse to whom he doth belong;
Let him (quoth Gam) but if't be not to me,
For any right you have, he may goe free.

With that couragious Morrisby grew hot,
Were not said he his Ransome worth a pin,
Now by these Armes I weare thou gett'st him not:
Or if thou do'st, thou shalt him hardly win;
Gam whose Welch blood could hardly brooke this blot,
To bend his Axe upon him doth begin:
He his at him, till the Lord Beamount came
Their rash attempt, and wisely thus doth blame.

Are not the French twice trebl'd to our power,
And fighting still, nay, doubtfull yet the day:
Thinke you not these us fast enough deuoure:
But that your braves the Army must dismay:
If ought but good befell us in this howre:
This be you sure your lyues for it must pay:
Then first the end of this dayes Battaile see,
And then decide whose prisoner he shall be.

Now Excester with his untaynted Reare
Came on, which long had labour'd to come in:
And with the Kings mayne Battell up doth beare;
Who still kept off, till the last houre had bin:
He cryes and clamours ev'ry way doth heare:
But yet he knew not which the day should win:
Nor askes of any what were fit to doe,
But where the French were thick'st, he falleth to.

The Earle of Vandom certainly that thought,
The English fury somewhat had beene stayde:
Weary with slaughter as men over-wrought,

Nor had beene spurr'd on by a second ayde:
For his owne safety, then more fiercely fought,
Hoping the tempest somewhat had been layde:
And he thereby (though suff'ring the defeate,)
Might keep his Reareward whole in his Retreate.

On whom the Duke of Excester then fell,
Reare with the Reare now for their Valours vy,
Ours finde the French their lyues will dearely sell;
And th'English meane as dearely them to buy:
The English follow, should they runne through hell,
And through the same the French must, if they flye,
When too't they goe, deciding it with blowes,
With th'one side now, then with th'other't goes.

But the sterne English with such luck and might,
(As though the Fates had sworne to take their parts)
Upon the French preuailing in the Fight,
With doubled hands, and with re-doubled harts,
The more in perill still the more in plight,
Gainst them whom Fortune miserably thwarts:
Disabled quite before the Foe to stand,
But fall like grasse before the Mowers hand.

That this French Earle is beaten on the Field,
His fighting Souldiers round about him slaine;
And when himselfe a Prisoner he would yeeld,
And beg'd for life, it was but all in vaine;
Their Bills the English doe so easely weeld
To kill the French, as though it were no paine;
For this to them was their auspicious day,
The more the English fight, the more they may.

When now the Marshall Boucequalt, which long
Had through the Battaile waded ev'ry way,
Oft hazarded the murther'd Troupes among,
Encouraging them to abide the day:
Finding the Army that he thought so strong,
Before the English faintly to dismay,
Brings on the wings which of the rest remain'd,
With which the Battaile stoutly he maintain'd.

Till olde Sir Thomas Erpingham at last,
With those three hundred Archers commeth in,
Which layd in ambush not three houres yet past;
Had the Defeat of the French Army bin,
With these that noble Souldier maketh hast,
Lest other from him should the honour win:

Who as before now stretch their well-wax'd strings,
At the French Horse then comming in the wings.

The soyle with slaughter ev'ry where they load,
Whilst the French stoutly to the English stood,
The drops from eithers emptied veynes that flow'd,
Where it was lately firme had made a flood:
But heau'n that day to the brave English ow'd;
The Sunne that rose in water, set in blood:
Nothing but horrour to be look'd for there,
And the stout Marshall vainely doth but feare.

His Horse sore wounded whilst he went aside,
To take another still that doth attend,
A shaft which some too-lucky hand doth guide,
Peircing his Gorget brought him to his end;
Which when the proud Lord Falkonbridge espide,
Thinking from thence to beare away his friend,
Strucke from his Horse, with many a mortall wound,
Is by the English nayled to the ground.

The Marshalls death so much doth them affright,
That downe their weapons instantly they lay,
And better yet to fit them for their flight,
Their weightier Armes, they wholly cast away,
Their hearts so heauy, makes their heeles so light,
That there was no intreating them to stay,
Ore hedge and ditch distractedly they take,
And happiest he, that greatest haste could make.

When Vadamount now in the Conflict mett,
With valient Brabant, whose high valour showne
That day, did many a blunted Courage whett,
Else long before that from the Field had flowne,
Quoth Vadamount, see how we are besett,
To death like to be troden by our owne,
My Lord of Brabant, what is to be done?
See how the French before the English runne.

Why, let them runne and neuer turne the head,
Quoth the brave Duke, untill their hatefull breath
Forsake their Bodies, and so farre have fled,
That France be not disparadg'd by their death:
Who trusts to Cowards ne'r is better sped,
Be he accurst, with such that holdeth faith,
Slaughter consume the Recreants as they flye,
Branded with shame, so basely may they dye.

Ignoble French, your fainting Cowardize craves
The dreadfull curse of your owne Mother earth,
Hardning her breast, not to allow you graves,
Be she so much ashamed of your birth;
May he be curst that one of you but saues,
And be in France hereafter such a dearth
Of Courage, that men from their wits it feare,
A Drumme, or Trumpet when they hap to heare.

From Burgundy brought I the force I had,
To fight for them, that ten from one doe flye;
It splits my breast, O that I could be mad;
To vexe these Slaues who would not dare to dye:
In all this Army is there not a Lad,
Th'ignoble French for Cowards that dare crye:
If scarse one found, then let me be that one,
The English Army that oppos'd alone.

This said, he puts his Horse upon his speed,
And in, like lightning on the English flewe:
Where many a Mothers sonne he made to bleed,
Whilst him with much astonishment they viewe:
Where having acted many a Knight-like deed,
Him and his Horse they all to peeces hewe:
Yet he that day more lasting glory wan,
Except Alanzon then did any man.

When as report to great King Henry came,
Of a vast Route which from the Battaile fled,
(Amongst the French most men of speciall name)
By the stout English fiercely followed;
Had for their safety, (much though to their shame)
Got in their flight into so strong a sted,
So fortifi'd by nature (as 'twas thought)
They might not thence, but with much blood be brought.

An aged Rampire, with huge Ruines heapt,
Which seru'd for Shot, gainst those that should assayle,
Whose narrow entrance they with Crosbowes kept,
Whose sharpned quarres came in show'rs like hayle:
Quoth the brave King, first let the field be swept,
And with the rest we well enough shall deale;
Which though some heard, and so shut up their eare,
Yet relish'd not with many Souldiers there.

Some that themselves by Ransomes would enrich,
(To make their pray of Pesants yet dispise)
Felt as they thought their bloody palmes to itch,

To be in action for their wealthy prize:
Others whom onely glory doth bewitch,
Rather then life would to this enterprize:
Most men seem'd willing, yet not any one
Would put himselfe this great exployt upon.

Which Woodhouse hearing meerily thus spake,
(One that right well knew, both his worth and wit)
A dangerous thing it is to undertake
A Fort, where Souldiers be defending it,
Perhaps they sleepe, and if they should awake,
With stones, or with their shafts they may us hitt,
And in our Conquest whilst so well we fare,
It were meere folly, but I see none dare.

Which Gam o'r hearing (being neere at hand)
Not dare quoth he, and angerly doth frowne,
I tell thee Woodhouse, some in presence stand,
Dare propp the Sunne if it were falling downe,
Dare graspe the bolt from Thunder in his hand,
And through a Cannon leape into a Towne;
I tell thee, a resolued man may doe
Things, that thy thoughts, yet neuer mounted to.

I know that resolution may doe much,
Woodhouse replyes, but who could act my thought,
With his proud head the Pole might easely tuch,
And Gam quoth he, though bravely thou hast fought,
Yet not the fame thou hast attain'd too, such,
But that behind, as great is to be bought,
And yonder tis, then Gam come up with me,
Where soone the King our Courages shall see.

Agreed quoth Gam, and up their Troopes they call,
Hand over head, and on the French they ran,
And to the fight couragiously they fall,
When on both sides the slaughter soone began;
Fortune awhile indifferent is to all,
These what they may, and those doe what they can.
Woodhouse and Gam, upon each other vye,
By Armes their manhood desperatly to try.

To clime the Fort the Light-Arm'd English striue,
And some by Trees there growing to ascend;
The French with Flints let at the English driue,
Themselves with Shields the Englishmen defend,
And faine the Fort downe with their hands would riue:
Thus either side their vtmost power extend,

Till valiant Gam sore wounded, drawne aside
By his owne Souldiers, shortly after dy'de.

Then take they up the bodies of the slaine,
Which for their Targets ours before them beare,
And with a fresh assault come on againe;
Scarse in the Field yet, such a fight as there,
Crosse-bowes, and Long-bowes at it are amaine,
Until the French their massacre that feare,
Of the fierce English, a cessation craue,
Offring to yeeld, so they their lives would saue.

Lewis of Burbon in the furious heat
Of this great Battaile, having made some stay,
Who with the left wing suffered a defeate,
In the beginning of this lucklesse day,
Finding the English forcing their retreat,
And that much hope upon his valour lay,
Fearing lest he might undergoe some shame,
That were unworthy of the Burbon name.

Hath gathered up some scattred Troopes of Horse,
That in the Field stood doubtfull what to doe;
Though with much toyle, which he doth reinforce
With some small power that he doth add thereto,
Proclaiming still the English had the worse,
And now at last, with him if they would goe,
He dares assure them Victory, if not
The greatest fame that euer Souldiers gott.

And being wise, so Burbon to beguile
The French, (preparing instantly to fly)
Procures a Souldier, by a secret wile
To come in swiftly and to craue supply,
That if with Courage they would fight awhile,
It certaine was the English all should dye,
For that the King had offered them to yeeld,
Finding his troopes to leaue him on the Field.

When Arthur Earle of Richmount comming in,
With the right wing that long staid out of sight,
Having too lately with the English bin,
But finding Burbon bent againe to fight,
His former credit hoping yet to winn,
(Which at that instant easily he might)
Comes close up with him, and puts on as fast,
Bravely resolu'd to fight it to the last.

And both encourag'd by the newes was braught
Of the ariuing of the Daulphins power;
Whose speedy Van, their Reare had almost raught,
(From Agincourt discover'd from a Tower)
Which with the Norman Gallantry was fraught,
And on the suddaine comming like a shower;
Would bring a deluge on the English Host,
Whilst they yet stood their victory to boast.

And one they come, as doth a rowling tide,
Forc'd by a winde, that shoues it forth so fast,
Till it choke up some chanell side to side,
And the craz'd banks doth downe before it cast,
Hoping the English would them not abide,
Or would be so amazed at their hast,
That should they faile to route them at their will,
Yet of their blood, the fields should drinke their fill.

When as the English whose o'r-wearied Armes,
Were with long slaughter lately waxed sore,
These inexpected, and so fierce Alarmes,
To their first strength doe instantly restore,
And like a Stoue their stifned sinewes warmes,
To act as bravely as they did before;
And the proud French as stoutly to oppose,
Scorning to yeeld one foot despight of blowes.

The fight is fearefull, for stout Burbon brings
His fresher forces on with such a shocke,
That they were like to cut the Archers strings
E're they their Arrowes hansomly could nock
The French like Engines that were made with springs:
Themselves so fast into the English lock,
That th'one was like the other downe to beare,
In wanting roomth to strike, they stoode so neare.

Still staggering long they from each other reel'd,
Glad that themselves they so could disingage:
And falling back upon the spacious field
(For this last Sceane, that is the bloody Stage)
Where they their Weapons liberally could weeld,
They with such madnesse execute their rage;
As though the former fury of the day,
To this encounter had but beene a play.

Slaughter is now desected to the full,
Here from their backs their batter'd Armours fall,
Here a sleft shoulder, there a cloven scull,

There hang his eyes out beaten with a mall,
Untill the edges of their Bills growe dull,
Upon each other they so spend their gall,
Wilde showtes and clamors all the ayre doe fill,
The French cry tue, and the English kill.

The Duke of Barre in this vaste spoyle by chance;
With the Lord Saint-Iohn on the Field doth meete,
Towards whom that brave Duke doth himselfe aduance,
Who with the like encounter him doth greete:
This English Barron, and this Peere of France,
Grapling together, falling from their feete,
With the rude crowdes had both to death beene crusht,
In for their safety, had their friends not rusht.

Both againe rais'd, and both their Souldiers shift,
To saue their lyues if any way they could:
But as the French the Duke away would lift,
Upon his Armes the English taking hould,
(Men of that sort, that thought upon their thrift)
Knowing his Ransome dearely would be sould:
Dragge him away in spight of their defence,
Which to their Quarter would have borne him thence.

Meane while brave Burbon from his stirring Horse,
Gall'd with an Arrow to the earth is throwne;
By a meane Souldier seased on by force,
Hoping to have him certainly his owne,
Which this Lord holdeth better so then worse:
Since the French fortune to that ebbe is growne,
And he perceiues the Souldier him doth deeme,
To be a person of no meane esteeme.

Berckley and Burnell, two brave English Lords,
Flesht with French blood, and in their Valours pride,
Aboue their Arm'd heads brandishing their swords,
As they tryumphing through the Army ride,
Finding what prizes Fortune here affords
To ev'ry Souldier, and more wistly eyde
This gallant prisoner, by his Arming see,
Of the great Burbon family to be.

And from the Souldier they his Prisoner take,
Of which the French Lord seemeth wondrous faine
Thereby his safety more secure to make:
Which when the Souldier findes his hopes in vaine,
So rich a Booty forced to forsake,
To put himselfe, and prisoner out of paine:

He on the suddaine stabs him, and doth sweare,
Would th'aue his Ransome, they should take it there.

When Rosse and Morley making in amaine,
Bring the Lord Darcy up with them along,
Whose Horse had lately under him beene slaine;
And they on foote found fighting in the throng,
Those Lords his friends remounting him againe,
Being a man that valiant was and strong:
They altogether with a generall hand,
Charge on the French that they could finde to stand.

And yet but vainely as the French suppos'd,
For th'Earle of Richmount forth such earth had found,
That one two sides with quick-set was enclos'd,
And the way to it by a rising ground,
By which a while the English were oppos'd,
At every Charge which else came up so round,
As that except the passage put them by,
The French as well might leaue their Armes and flye.

Upon both parts it furiously is fought,
And with such quicknesse riseth to that hight,
That horror neede no further to be sought:
If onely that might satisfie the sight,
Who would have fame full dearely here it bought,
For it was sold by measure and by waight,
And at one rate the price still certaine stood,
An ounce of honour cost a pound of blood.

When so it hapt that Dampier in the Van,
Meetes with stout Darcy, but whilst him he prest,
Over and over commeth horse and man,
Of whom the other soone himselfe possest:
When as Sauesses upon Darcy ran
To ayde Dampier, but as he him adrest;
A Halbert taking hold upon his Greaues,
Him from his Saddle violently heaues.

When soone fiue hundred Englishmen at Armes,
That to the French had given many a chase;
And when they covered all the Field with swarmes;
Yet oft that day had bravely bid them base:
Now at the last by raising fresh Alarmes;
And comming up with an unusuall pace,
Made them to knowe, that they must runne or yeeld,
Neuer till now the English had the Field.

Where Arthur Earle of Richmount beaten downe,
Is left (suppos'd of ev'ry one for dead)
But afterwards awaking from his swoone,
By some that found him, was recovered:
So Count Du Marle was likewise overthrowne:
As he was turning meaning to have fled,
Who fights, the colde blade in his bosome feeles,
Who flyes, still heares it whisking at his heeles.

Till all disrank'd, like seely Sheepe they runne,
By threats nor prayers, to be constrain'd to stay;
For that their hearts were so extreamely done,
That fainting oft they fall upon the way:
Or when they might a present perill shunne,
They rush upon it by their much dismay,
That from the English should they safely flye,
Of their owne very feare, yet they should dye.

Some they take prisoners, other some they kill,
As they affect those upon whom they fall:
For they as Victors may doe what they will:
For who this Conqueror to account dare call,
In gore the English seeme their soules to swill,
And the deiected French must suffer all;
Flight, cords, and slaughter, are the onely three,
To which themselves subiected they doe see.

A shoolesse Souldier there a man might meete,
Leading his Mounsier by the armes fast bound:
Another, his had shackled by the feete;
Who like a Cripple shuffled on the ground;
Another three or foure before him beete,
Like harmefull Chattell driuen to a pound;
They must abide it, so the Victor will,
Who at his pleasure may, or saue, or kill.

That brave French Gallant, when the fight began,
Who lease of Lackies ambled by his side,
Himselfe a Lacky now most basely ran,
Whilst a rag'd Souldier on his Horse doth ride,
That Rascall is no lesse then at his man,
Who was but lately to his Luggadge tide;
And the French Lord now courtsies to that slaue,
Who the last day his Almes was like to craue.

And those few English wounded in the fight,
They force the French to bring with them away,
Who when they were depressed with the weight,

Yet dar'd not once their burthen downe to lay,
Those in the morne, whose hopes were at their height,
Are fallne thus lowe ere the departing day;
With pickes of Halberts prickt in steed of goads,
Like tyred Horses labouring with their Loads.

But as the English from the Field returne,
Some of those French who when the Fight began,
Forsooke their friends, and hoping yet to earne,
Pardon, for that so cowardly they ran,
Assay the English Carridges to burne,
Which to defend them scarsely had a man;
For that their keepers to the field were got,
To picke such spoyles, as chance should them alott.

The Captaines of this Rascall cowardly Route,
Were Isambert of Agincourt at hand,
Riflant of Clunasse a Dorpe there about,
And for the Chiefe in this their base command,
Was Robinett of Burnivile; throughout
The Countrie knowne, all order to withstand,
These with fiue hundred Peasants they had rais'd
The English Tents, upon an instant seas'd.

For setting on those with the Luggadge left,
A few poore Sutlers with the Campe that went,
They basely fell to pillage and to theft,
And having rifled every Booth and Tent,
Some of the sillyest they of life bereft,
The feare of which, some of the other sent,
Into the Army, with their suddaine cries,
Which put the King in feare of fresh supplies.

For that his Souldiers tyred in the fight,
Their Prisoners more in number then they were,
He thought it for a thing of too much weight,
T'oppose freshe forces, and to guard them there.
The Daulphins Powers, yet standing in their sight,
And Burbons Forces of the field not cleere.
These yearning cryes, that from the Caridge came,
His bloud yet hott, more highly doth inflame

And in his rage he instantly commands,
That every English should his prisoner kill,
Except some fewe in some great Captaines hands
Whose Ransomes might his emptyed Cofers fill,
Alls one whose loose, or who is nowe in bonds,
Both must one way, it is the Conquerers will.

Those who late thought, small Ransoms them might free
Saw onely death their Ransomes now must be.

Accursed French, and could it not suffize,
That ye but now bath'd in your natiue gore;
But yee must thus infortunately rise,
To drawe more plagues upon yee then before,
And gainst your selfe more mischeife to diuise,
Then th'English could have, and set wide the dore.
To vtter ruine, and to make an end
Of that your selves, which others would not spend.

Their vtmost rage the English now had breath'd,
And their proud heartes gan somewhat to relent,
Their bloody swords they quietly had sheath'd,
And their strong bowes already were unbent,
To easefull rest their bodies they bequeath'd,
Nor farther harme at all to you they ment,
And to that paynes must yee them needsly putt,
To draw their kniues once more your throats to cutt.

That French who lately by the English stood,
And freely ask'd what ransome he should pay,
Whoe somwhat coold, and in a calmer moode,
Agreed with him both of the some and day,
Nowe findes his flesh must be the present foode,
For wolues and Rauens, for the same that stay.
And sees his blood on th'others sword to flowe,
E'r his quicke sense could aprehend the blowe.

Whilst one is asking what the bus'nesse is,
Hearing (in French) his Country-man to crye:
He who detaines him prisoner, answers this:
Mounsier, the King commands that you must dye;
This is plaine English, whilst he's killing his:
He sees another on a French man flye,
And with a Poleax pasheth out his braines,
Whilst he's demanding what the Garboyle meanes.

That tender heart whose chance it was to have,
Some one, that day who did much valour showe,
Who might perhaps have had him for his Slaue:
But equall Lots had Fate pleas'd to bestowe:
He who his prisoner willingly would saue,
Lastly constrain'd to give the deadly blowe
That sends him downe to euerlasting sleepe:
Turning his face, full bitterly doth weepe.

Ten thousand French that inwardly were well,
Saue some light hurts that any man might heale:
Euen at an instant, in a minute fell,
And their owne friends their deathes to them to deale.
Yet of so many, very fewe could tell,
Nor could the English perfectly reueale,
The desperate cause of this disastrous hap,
That euen as Thunder kill'd them with a clap.

How happy were those in the very hight,
Of this great Battaile, that had bravely dyde,
When as their boyling bosomes in the fight,
Felt not the sharpe steele thorough them to slide:
But these now in a miserable plight,
Must in cold blood this massacre abide,
Caus'd by those Villaines (curst alive and dead,)
That from the field the passed morning fled.

When as the King to Crowne this glorious day,
Now bids his Souldiers after all this toyle,
(No forces found that more might them dismay)
Of the dead French to take the gen'rall spoyle,
Whose heapes had well neere stopt up ev'ry way;
For eu'n as Clods they cov'red all the soyle,
Commanding none should any one controle,
Catch that catch might, but each man to his dole.

They fall to groping busily for gold,
Of which about them the slaine French had store,
They finde as much as well their hands can hold,
Who had but siluer, him they counted poore,
Scarfes, Chaines, and Bracelets, were not to be told,
So rich as these no Souldiers were before;
Who got a Ring would scarsly put it on,
Except therein there were some Radiant stone.

Out of rich sutes the Noblest French they strip,
And leaue their Bodies naked on the ground,
And each one fills his Knapsack or his Scrip;
With some rare thing that on the Field is found:
About his bus'nesse he doth nimbly skip,
That had upon him many a cruell wound:
And where they found a French not out-right slaine,
They him a prisoner constantly retaine.

Who scarse a Shirt had but the day before,
Nor a whole Stocking to keepe out the cold,
Hath a whole Wardrop (at command in store)

In the French fashion flaunting it in gold,
And in the Tauerne, in his Cups doth rore,
Chocking his Crownes, and growes thereby so bold,
That proudly he a Captaines name assumes,
In his gilt Gorget with his tossing Plumes.

Waggons and Carts are laden till they crackt,
With Armes and Tents there taken in the Field;
For want of carridge on whose tops are packt,
Ensignes, Coat-Armours, Targets, Speares, and Shields:
Nor neede they conuoy, fearing to be sackt;
For all the Country to King Henry yeelds,
And the poore Pesant helpes along to beare,
What late the goods of his proud Landlord were.

A Horse well furnisht for a present Warre:
For a French Crowne might any where be bought,
But if so be that he had any scarre,
Though ne'r so small, he valew'd was at naught;
With spoyles so sated the proud English are;
Amongst the slaine, that who for pillage sought,
Except some rich Caparizon he found,
For a steele Saddle would not stoupe to ground.

And many a hundred beaten downe that were,
Whose wounds were mortall, others wondrous deepe,
When as the English over-past they heare:
And no man left a Watch on them to keepe,
Into the Bushes, and the Ditches neare,
Upon their weake hands and their knees doe creepe:
But for their hurts tooke ayre, and were undrest,
They were found dead, and buried with the rest.

Thus when the King sawe that the Coast was clear'd,
And of the French who were not slaine were fled:
Nor in the Field not any then appear'd,
That had the power againe to make a head:
This Conquerour exceedingly is cheer'd,
Thanking his God that he so well had sped,
And so tow'rds Callice bravely marching on,
Leaueth sad France her losses to bemoane.

FINIS.

Michael Drayton – A Short Biography by Cyril Brett

Michael Drayton was born in 1563, at Hartshill, near Atherstone, in Warwickshire.

He became a page to Sir Henry Goodere, at Polesworth Hall: his own words give the best picture of his early years here. His education would seem to have been good, but ordinary; and it is very doubtful if he ever went to a university. Besides the authors mentioned in the Epistle to Henry Reynolds, he was certainly familiar with Ovid and Horace, and possibly with Catullus: while there seems no reason to doubt that he read Greek, though it is quite true that his references to Greek authors do not prove any first-hand acquaintance. He understood French, and read Rabelais and the French sonneteers, and he seems to have been acquainted with Italian. His knowledge of English literature was wide, and his judgement good: but his chief bent lay towards the history, legendary and otherwise, of his native country, and his vast stores of learning on this subject bore fruit in the Poly-Olbion.

While still at Polesworth, Drayton fell in love with his patron's younger daughter, Anne; and, though she married, in 1596, Sir Henry Raynsford of Clifford, Drayton continued his devotion to her for many years, and also became an intimate friend of her husband's, writing a sincere elegy on his death.

About February, 1591, Drayton paid a visit to London, and published his first work, the Harmony of the Church, a series of paraphrases from the Old Testament, in fourteen-syllabled verse of no particular vigour or grace. This book was immediately suppressed by order of Archbishop Whitgift, possibly because it was supposed to savour of Puritanism. The author, however, published another edition in 1610; indeed, he seems to have had a fondness for this style of work; for in 1604 he published a dull poem, Moyses in a Map of his Miracles, re-issued in 1630 as Moses his Birth and Miracles. Accompanying this piece, in 1630, were two other 'Divine poems': Noah's Floud, and David and Goliath. Noah's Floud is, in part, one of Drayton's happiest attempts at the catalogue style of bestiary; and Mr. Elton finds in it some foreshadowing of the manner of Paradise Lost. But, as a whole, Drayton's attempts in this direction deserve the oblivion into which they, in common with the similar productions of other authors, have fallen. In the dedication and preface to the Harmony of the Church are some of the few traces of Euphuism shown in Drayton's work; passages in the Heroical Epistles also occur to the mind He was always averse to affectation, literary or otherwise, and in Elegy VIII deliberately condemns Lyly's fantastic style.

Probably before Drayton went up to London, Sir Henry Goodere saw that he would stand in need of a patron more powerful than the master of Polesworth, and introduced him to the Earl and Countess of Bedford. Those who believe Drayton to have been a Pope in petty spite, identify the 'Idea' of his earlier poems with Lucy, Countess of Bedford; though they are forced to acknowledge as self-evident that the 'Idea' of his later work is Anne, Lady Raynsford. They then proceed to say that Drayton, after consistently honouring the Countess in his verse for twelve years, abruptly transferred his allegiance, not forgetting to heap foul abuse on his former patroness, out of pique at some temporary withdrawal of favour. Not only is this directly contrary to all we know and can infer of Drayton's character, but Mr. Elton has decisively disproved it by a summary of bibliographical and other evidence. Into the question it is here unnecessary to enter, and it has been mentioned only because it alone, of the many Drayton-controversies, has cast any slur on the poet's reputation.

In 1593, Drayton published Idea, the Shepherds Garland, in nine Eclogues; in 1606 he added a tenth, the best of all, to the new edition, and rearranged the order, so that the new eclogue became the ninth. In these Pastorals, while following the Shepherds Calendar in many ways, he already displays something of the sturdy independence which characterized him through life. He abandons Spenser's quasi-rustic dialect, and, while keeping to most of the pastoral conventions, such as the singing-match and threnody, he contrives to introduce something of a more natural and homely strain. He keeps the political allusions, notably in the Eclogue containing the song in praise of Beta, who is, of course, Queen Elizabeth. But an over-bold remark in the last line of that song was struck out in 1606; and the new eclogue has no political reference. He is not ashamed to allude directly to Spenser; and indeed his direct debts are limited to a few scattered phrases, as in the Ballad of Dowsabel. Almost to the end of his literary career, Drayton mentions Spenser with reverence and praise.

It is in the songs interspersed in the Eclogues that Drayton's best work at this time is to be found: already his metrical versatility is discernible; for though he doubtless remembered the many varieties of metre employed by Spenser in the Calendar, his verses already bear a stamp of their own. The long but impetuous lines, such as 'Trim up her golden tresses with Apollo's sacred tree', afford a striking contrast to the archaic romance-metre, derived from Sir Thopas and its fellows, which appears in Dowsabel, and it again to the melancholy, murmuring cadences of the lament for Elphin. It must, however, be confessed that certain of the songs in the 1593 edition were full of recondite conceits and laboured antitheses, and were rightly struck out, to be replaced by lovelier poems, in the edition of 1606. The song to Beta was printed in Englands Helicon, 1600; here, for the first time, appeared the song of Dead Love, and for the only time, Rowlands Madrigal. In these songs, Drayton offends least in grammar, always a weak point with him; in the body of the Eclogues, in the earlier Sonnets, in the Odes, occur the most extraordinary and perplexing inversions. Quite the most striking feature of the Eclogues, especially in their later form, is their bold attempt at greater realism, at a breaking-away from the conventional images and scenery.

Having paid his tribute to one poetic fashion, Drayton in 1594 fell in with the prevailing craze for sonneteering, and published Ideas Mirrour, a series of fifty-one 'amours' or sonnets, with two prefatory poems, one by Drayton and one by an unknown, signing himself Gorbo il fidele. The title of these poems Drayton possibly borrowed from the French sonneteer, de Pontoux: in their style much recollection of Sidney, Constable, and Daniel is traceable. They are ostensibly addressed to his mistress, and some of them are genuine in feeling; but many are merely imitative exercises in conceit; some, apparently, trials in metre. These amours were again printed, with the title of 'sonnets', in 1599, 1600, 1602, 1603, 1605, 1608, 1610, 1613, 1619, and 1631, during the poet's lifetime. It is needless here to discuss whether Drayton were the 'rival poet' to Shakespeare, whether these sonnets were really addressed to a man, or merely to the ideal Platonic beauty; for those who are interested in these points, I subjoin references to the sonnets which touch upon them. From the prentice-work evident in many of the Amours, it would seem that certain of them are among Drayton's earliest poems; but others show a craftsman not meanly advanced in his art. Nevertheless, with few exceptions, this first 'bundle of sonnets' consists rather of trials of skill, bubbles of the mind; most of his sonnets which strike the reader as touched or penetrated with genuine passion belong to the editions from 1599 onwards; implying that his love for Anne Goodere, if at all represented in these poems, grew with his years, for the 'love-parting' is first found in the edition of 1619. But for us the question should not be, are these sonnets genuine representations of the personal feeling of the poet? but rather, how far do they arouse or echo in us as individuals the universal passion? There are at least some of Drayton's sonnets which possess a direct, instant, and universal appeal, by reason of their simple force and straightforward ring; and not in virtue of any subtle charm of sound and rhythm, or overmastering splendour of diction or thought. Ornament vanishes, and soberness and simplicity increase, as we proceed in the editions of the sonnets. Drayton's chief attempt in the jewelled or ornamental style appeared in 1595, with the title of Endimion and Phoebe, and was, in a sense, an imitation of Marlowe's Hero and Leander. Hero and Leander is, as Swinburne says, a shrine of Parian marble, illuminated from within by a clear flame of passion; while Endimion and Phoebe is rather a curiously wrought tapestry, such as that in Mortimer's Tower, woven in splendid and harmonious colours, wherein, however, the figures attain no clearness or subtlety of outline, and move in semiconventional scenery. It is, none the less, graceful and impressive, and of a like musical fluency with other poems of its class, such as Venus and Adonis, or Salmacis and Hermaphrodius. Parts of it were reset and spoilt in a 1606 publication of Drayton's, called The Man in the Moone.

In 1593 and 1594 Drayton also published his earliest pieces on the mediaeval theme of the 'Falls of the Illustrious'; they were Peirs Gavesson and Matilda the faire and chaste daughter of the Lord Robert Fitzwater. Here Drayton followed in the track of Boccaccio, Lydgate, and the Mirrour for Magistrates, walking in the way which Chaucer had derided in his Monkes Tale: and with only too great fidelity does Drayton adapt himself to the dullnesses of his model: fine rhetoric is not altogether wanting, and there is, of course, the consciousness that these subjects deal with the history of his beloved country, but neither these, nor Robert, Duke of Normandy (1596), nor Great Cromwell, Earl of Essex (1607 and 1609), nor the Miseries of Margaret (1627) can escape the charge of tediousness. England's Heroical Epistles were first published in 1597, and other editions, of 1598, 1599, and 1602, contain new epistles. These are Drayton's first attempt to strike out a new and original vein of English poetry: they are a series of letters, modelled on Ovid's Heroides, addressed by various pairs of lovers, famous in English history, to each other, and arranged in chronological order, from Henry II and Rosamond to Lady Jane Grey and Lord Guilford Dudley. They are, in a sense, the most important of Drayton's writings, and they have certainly been the most popular, up to the early nineteenth century. In these poems Drayton foreshadowed, and probably inspired, the smooth style of Fairfax, Waller, and Dryden. The metre, the grammar, and the thought, are all perfectly easy to follow, even though he employs many of the Ovidian 'turns' and 'clenches'. A certain attempt at realization of the different characters is observable, but the poems are fine rhetorical exercises rather than realizations of the dramatic and passionate possibilities of their themes. In 1596, Drayton, as we have seen, published the Mortimeriados, a kind of epic, with Mortimer as its hero, of the wars between King Edward II and the Barons. It was written in the seven-line stanza of Chaucer's Troilus and Cressida and Spenser's Hymns. On its republication in 1603, with the title of the Barons' Wars, the metre was changed to ottava rima, and Drayton showed, in an excellent preface, that he fully appreciated the principles and the subtleties of the metrical art. While possessing many fine passages, the Barons' Wars is somewhat dull, lacking much of the poetry of the older version; and does not escape from Drayton's own criticism of Daniel's Chronicle Poems: 'too much historian in verse, ... His rhymes were smooth, his metres well did close, But yet his manner better fitted prose'. The description of Mortimer's Tower in the sixth book recalls the ornate style of Endimion and Phoebe, while the fifth book, describing the miseries of King Edward, is the most moving and dramatic. But there is a general lifelessness and lack of movement for which these purple passages barely atone. The cause of the production of so many chronicle poems about this time has been supposed to be the desire of showing the horrors of civil war, at a time when the queen was growing old, and no successor had, as it seemed, been accepted. Also they were a kind of parallel to the Chronicle Play; and Drayton, in any case even if we grant him to have been influenced by the example of Daniel, never needed much incentive to treat a national theme.

About this time, we find Drayton writing for the stage. It seems unnecessary here to discuss whether the writing of plays is evidence of Drayton's poverty, or his versatility; but the fact remains that he had a hand in the production of about twenty. Of these, the only one which certainly survives is The first part of the true and honorable historie, of the life of Sir John Oldcastle, the good Lord Cobham, &c. It is practically impossible to distinguish Drayton's share in this curious play, and it does not, therefore, materially assist the elucidation of the question whether he had any dramatic feeling or skill. It can be safely affirmed that the dramatic instinct was nor uppermost in his mind; he was a Seneca rather than a Euripides: but to deny him all dramatic idea, as does Dr. Whitaker, is too severe. There is decided, if slender, dramatic skill and feeling in certain of the Nymphals. Drayton's persons are usually, it must be said, rather figures in a tableau, or series of tableaux; but in the second and seventh Nymphals, and occasionally in the tenth, there is real dramatic movement. Closely connected with this question is the consideration of humour, which is wrongly denied to Drayton. Humour is observable first, perhaps, in the Owle (1604); then in the Ode to his Rival (1619); and later in the Nymphidia, Shepheards Sirena, and Muses Elyzium. The second Nymphal shows us the quiet laughter, the humorous twinkle, with which Drayton writes at times. The subject is an [Greek: agôn] or contest between two shepherds for the affections of a nymph called Lirope: Lalus is a vale-bred swain, of refined and elegant manners, skilled, nevertheless, in all manly sports and exercises; Cleon, no less a master in physical prowess, was nurtured by a hind in the mountains; the contrast between their manners is admirably sustained: Cleon is rough, inclined to be rude and scoffing, totally without tact, even where his mistress is concerned. Lalus remembers her upbringing and her tastes; he makes no unnecessary or ostentatious display of wealth; his gifts are simple and charming, while Cleon's are so grotesquely unsuited to a swain, that it is tempting to suppose that Drayton was quietly satirizing Marlowe's Passionate Shepherd. Lirope listens gravely to the swains in turn, and makes demure but provoking answers, raising each to the height of hope, and then casting them both down into the depths of despair; finally she refuses both, yet without altogether killing hope. Her first answer is a good specimen of her banter and of Drayton's humour.

On the accession of James I, Drayton hastened to greet the King with a somewhat laboured song To the Maiestie of King James; but this poem was apparently considered to be premature: he cried Vivat Rex, without having said, Mortua est eheu Regina, and accordingly he suffered the penalty of his 'forward pen', and was severely neglected by King and Court. Throughout James's reign a darker and more satirical mood possesses Drayton, intruding at times even into his strenuous recreation-ground, the Poly-Olbion, and manifesting itself more directly in his satires, the Owle (1604), the Moon-Calfe (1627), the Man in the Moone (1606), and his verse-letters and elegies; while his disappointment with the times, the country, and the King, flashes out occasionally even in the Odes, and is heard in his last publication, the Muses Elizium (1630). To counterbalance the disappointment in his hopes from the King, Drayton found a new and life-long friend in Walter Aston, of Tixall, in Staffordshire; this gentleman was created Knight of the Bath by James, and made Drayton one of his esquires. By Aston's 'continual bounty' the poet was able to devote himself almost entirely to more congenial literary work; for, while Meres speaks of the Poly-Olbion in 1598, and we may easily see that Drayton had the idea of that work at least as early as 1594, yet he cannot have been able to give much time to it till now. Nevertheless, the 'declining and corrupt times' worked on Drayton's mind and grieved and darkened his soul, for we must remember that he was perfectly prosperous then and was not therefore incited to satire by bodily want or distress.

In 1604 he published the Owle, a mild satire, under the form of a moral fable of government, reminding the reader a little of the Parlement of Foules. The Man in the Moone (1606) is partly a recension of Endimion and Phoebe, but is a heterogeneous mass of weakly satire, of no particular merit. The Moon-Calfe (1627) is Drayton's most savage and misanthropic excursion into the region of Satire; in which, though occasionally nobly ironic, he is more usually coarse and blustering, in the style of Marston. In 1605 Drayton brought out his first 'collected poems', from which the Eclogues and the Owle are omitted; and in 1606 he published his Poemes Lyrick and Pastorall, Odes, Eglogs, The Man in the Moone. Of these the Eglogs are a recension of the Shepherd's Garland of 1593: we have already spoken of The Man in the Moone. The Odes are by far the most important and striking feature of the book. In the preface, Drayton professes to be following Pindar, Anacreon, and Horace, though, as he modestly implies, at a great distance. Under the title of Odes he includes a variety of subjects, and a variety of metres; ranging from an Ode to his Harp or to his Criticks, to a Ballad of Agincourt, or a poem on the Rose compared with his Mistress. In the edition of 1619 appeared several more Odes, including some of the best; while many of the others underwent careful revision, notably the Ballad. 'Sing wee the Rose,' perhaps because of its unintelligibility, and the Ode to his friend John Savage, perhaps because too closely imitated from Horace, were omitted. Drayton was not the first to use the term Ode for a lyrical poem, in English: Soothern in 1584, and Daniel in 1592 had preceded him; but he was the first to give the name popularity in England, and to lift the kind as Ronsard had lifted it in France; and till the time of Cowper no other English poet showed mastery of the short, staccato measure of the Anacreontic as distinct from the Pindaric Ode. In the Odes Drayton shows to the fullest extent his metrical versatility: he touches the Skeltonic metre, the long ten-syllabled line of the Sacrifice to Apollo; and ascends from the smooth and melodious rhythms of the New Year through the inspiring harp-tones of the Virginian Voyage to the clangour and swing of the Ballad of Agincourt. His grammar is possibly more distorted here than anywhere, but, as Mr. Elton says, 'these are the obstacles of any poet who uses measures of four or six syllables.' His tone throughout is rather that of the harp, as played, perhaps, in Polesworth Hall, than that of any other instrument; but in 1619 Drayton has taken to him the lute of Carew and his compeers. In 1619 the style is lighter, the fancy gayer, more exquisite, more recondite. Most of his few metaphysical conceits are to be found in these later Odes, as in the Heart, the Valentine, and the Crier. In the comparison of the two editions the nobler, if more strained, tone of the earlier is obvious; it is still Elizabethan, in its nobility of ideal and purpose, in its enthusiasm, in its belief and confidence in England and her men; and this even though we catch a glimpse of the Jacobean woe in the Ode to John Savage: the 1619 Odes are of a different world; their spirit is lighter, more insouciant in appearance, though perhaps studiedly so; the rhythms are more fantastic, with less of strength and firmness, though with more of grace and superficial beauty; even the very textual alterations, while usually increasing the grace and the music of the lines, remind the reader that something of the old spontaneity and freshness is gone.

In 1607 and 1609, Drayton published two editions of the last and weakest of his mediaeval poems—the Legend of Great Cromwell; and for the next few years he produced nothing new, only attending to the publication of certain reprints and new editions. During this time, however, he was working steadily at the Poly-Olbion, helped by the patronage of Aston and of Prince Henry. In 1612-13, Drayton burst upon an indifferent world with the first part of the great poem, containing eighteen songs; the title-page will give the best idea of the contents and plan of the book: 'Poly-Olbion or a Chorographicall Description of the Tracts, Riuers, Mountaines, Forests, and other Parts of this renowned Isle of Great Britaine, With intermixture of the most Remarquable Stories, Antiquities, Wonders, Rarityes, Pleasures, and Commodities of the same: Digested in a Poem by Michael Drayton, Esq. With a Table added, for direction to those occurrences of Story and Antiquities, whereunto the Course of the Volume easily leades not.' &c. On this work Drayton had been engaged for nearly the whole of his poetical career. The learning and research displayed in the poem are extraordinary, almost equalling the erudition of Selden in his Annotations to each Song. The first part was, for various reasons, a drug in the market, and Drayton found great difficulty in securing a publisher for the second part. But during the years from 1613 to 1622, he became acquainted with Drummond of Hawthornden through a common friend, Sir William Alexander of Menstry, afterwards Earl of Stirling. In 1618, Drayton starts a correspondence; and towards the end of the year mentions that he is corresponding also with Andro Hart, bookseller, of Edinburgh. The subject of his letter was probably the publication of the Second Part; which Drayton alludes to in a letter of 1619 thus: 'I have done twelve books more, that is from the eighteenth book, which was Kent, if you note it; all the East part and North to the river Tweed; but it lies by me; for the booksellers and I are in terms; they are a company of base knaves, whom I both scorn and kick at.' Finally, in 1622, Drayton got Marriott, Grismand, and Dewe, of London, to take the work, and it was published with a dedication to Prince Charles, who, after his brother's death, had given Drayton patronage. Drayton's preface to the Second Part is well worth quoting:

'To any that will read it. When I first undertook this Poem, or, as some very skilful in this kind have pleased to term it, this Herculean labour, I was by some virtuous friends persuaded, that I should receive much comfort and encouragement therein; and for these reasons; First, that it was a new, clear, way, never before gone by any; then, that it contained all the Delicacies, Delights, and Rarities of this renowned Isle, interwoven with the Histories of the Britons, Saxons, Normans, and the later English: And further that there is scarcely any of the Nobility or Gentry of this land, but that he is in some way or other by his Blood interested therein. But it hath fallen out otherwise; for instead of that comfort, which my noble friends (from the freedom of their spirits) proposed as my due, I have met with barbarous ignorance, and base detraction; such a cloud hath the Devil drawn over the world's judgment, whose opinion is in few years fallen so far below all ballatry, that the lethargy is incurable: nay, some of the Stationers, that had the selling of the First Part of this Poem, because it went not so fast away in the sale, as some of their beastly and abominable trash, (a shame both to our language and nation) have either despitefully left out, or at least carelessly neglected the Epistles to the Readers, and so have cozened the buyers with unperfected books; which these that have undertaken the Second Part, have been forced to amend in the First, for the small number that are yet remaining in their hands. And some of our outlandish, unnatural, English, (I know not how otherwise to express them) stick not to say that there is nothing in this Island worth studying for, and take a great pride to be ignorant in any thing thereof; for these, since they delight in their folly, I wish it may be hereditary from them to their posterity, that their children may be begg'd for fools to the fifth generation, until it may be beyond the memory of man to know that there was ever other of their families: neither can this deter me from going on with Scotland, if means and time do not hinder me, to perform as much as I have promised in my First Song:

Till through the sleepy main, to Thuly I have gone,
And seen the Frozen Isles, the cold Deucalidon,
Amongst whose iron Rocks, grim Saturn yet remains
Bound in those gloomy caves with adamantine chains.

And as for those cattle whereof I spake before, Odi profanum vulgus, et arceo, of which I account them, be they never so great, and so I leave them. To my friends, and the lovers of my labours, I wish all happiness.
Michael Drayton.'

The Poly-Olbion as a whole is easy and pleasant to read; and though in some parts it savours too much of a mere catalogue, yet it has many things truly poetical. The best books are perhaps the XIII, XIV and XV, where he is on his own ground, and therefore naturally at his best. It is interesting to notice how much attention and space he devotes to Wales. He describes not only the 'wonders' but also the fauna and flora of each district; and of the two it would seem that the flowers interested him more. Though he was a keen observer of country sights and sounds (a fact sufficiently attested by the Nymphidia and the Nymphals), it is evident that his interest in most things except flowers was rather momentary or conventional than continuous and heart-felt; but of the flowers he loves to talk, whether he weaves us a garland for the Thame's wedding, or gives us the contents of a maund of simples; and his love, if somewhat homely and unimaginative, is apparent enough. But the main inspiration, as it is the main theme, of the Poly-Olbion is the glory and might and wealth, past, present, and future, of England, her possessions and her folk. Through all this glory, however, we catch the tone of Elizabethan sorrow over the 'Ruines of Time'; grief that all these mighty men and their works will perish and be forgotten, unless the poet makes them live for ever on the lips of men. Drayton's own voluminousness has defeated his purpose, and sunk his poem by its own bulk. Though it is difficult to go so far as Mr. Bullen, and say that the only thing better than a stroll in the Poly-Olbion is one in a Sussex lane, it is still harder to agree with Canon Beeching, that 'there are few beauties on the road', the beauties are many, though of a quietly rural type, and the road, if long and winding, is of good surface, while its cranks constitute much of its charm. It is doubtless, from the outside, an appalling poem in these days of epitomes and monographs, but it certainly deserves to be rescued from oblivion and read.

In 1618 Drayton contributed two Elegies to Henry FitzGeoffrey's Satyrs and Epigrames. These were on the Lady Penelope Clifton, and on 'the death of the three sonnes of the Lord Sheffield, drowned neere where Trent falleth into Humber'. Neither is remarkable save for far-fetched conceits; they were reprinted in 1610, and again, with many others, in the volume of 1627. In 1619 Drayton issued a folio collected edition of his works, and reprinted it in 1620. In 1627 followed a folio of wholly fresh matter, including the Battaile of Agincourt; the Miseries of Queene Margarite, Nimphidia, Quest of Cinthia, Shepheards Sirena, Moone-Calfe, and Elegies upon sundry occasions. The Battaile of Agincourt is a somewhat otiose expansion, with purple patches, of the Ballad; it is, nevertheless, Drayton's best lengthy piece on a historical theme. Of the Miseries of Queene Margarite and of the Moone-Calfe we have already spoken. The most notable piece in the book is the Nimphidia. This poem of the Court of Fairy has 'invention, grace, and humour', as Canon Beeching has said. It would be interesting to know exactly when it was composed and committed to paper, for it is thought that the three fairy poems in Herrick's Hesperides were written about 1626. In any case, Drayton's poem touches very little, and chiefly in the beginning, on the subject of any one of Herrick's three pieces. The style, execution, and impression left on the reader are quite different; even as they are totally unlike those of the Midsummer Night's Dream. Herrick's pieces are extraordinary combinations of the idea of 'King of Shadows', with a reality fantastically sober: the poems are steeped in moonlight. In Drayton all is clear day, or the most unromantic of nights; though everything is charming, there is no attempt at idealization, little of the higher faculty of imagination; but great realism, and much play of fancy. Herrick's verses were written by Cobweb and Moth together, Drayton's by Puck. Granting, however, the initial deficiency in subtlety of charm, the whole poem is inimitably graceful and piquant. The gay humour, the demure horror of the witchcraft, the terrible seriousness of the battle, wonderfully realize the mock-heroic gigantesque; and while there is not the minute accuracy of Gulliver in Lilliput, Drayton did not write for a sceptical or too-prying audience; quite half his readers believed more or less in fairies. In the metre of the poem Drayton again echoes that of the older romances, as he did in Dowsabel. In the Quest of Cinthia, while ostensibly we come to the real world of mortals, we are really in a non-existent land of pastoral convention, in the most pseudo-Arcadian atmosphere in which Drayton ever worked. The metre and the language are, however, charmingly managed. The Shepheards Sirena is a poem, apparently, 'where more is meant than meets the ear,' as so often in pastoral poetry; it is difficult to see exactly what is meant; but the Jacobean strain of doubt and fear is there, and the poem would seem to have been written some time earlier than 1627. The Elegies comprise a great variety of styles and themes; some are really threnodies, some verse-letters, some laments over the evil times, and one a summary of Drayton's literary opinions. He employs the couplet in his Elegies with a masterly hand, often with a deliberately rugged effect, as in his broader Marstonic satire addressed to William Browne; while the line of greater smoothness but equal strength is to be seen in the letters to Sandys and Jeffreys. He is fantastic and conceited in most of the threnodies; but, as is natural, that on his old friend, Sir Henry Raynsford, is least artificial and fullest of true feeling. The epistle to Henery Reynolds. Of Poets and Poesie shows Drayton as a sane and sagacious critic, ready to see the good, but keen to discern the weakness also; perhaps the clearest evidence of his critical skill is the way in which nearly all of his judgements on his contemporaries coincide with the received modern opinions.

In his later years Drayton enjoyed the patronage of the third Earl and Countess of Dorset; and in 1630 he published his last volume, the Muses Elizium, of which he dedicated the pastoral part to the Earl, and the three divine poems at the end to the Countess. The Muses Elizium proper consists of Ten Pastorals or Nymphals, prefaced by a Description of Elizium. The three divine poems have been mentioned before, and were Noah's Floud, Moses his Birth and Miracles, and David and Goliah. The Nymphals are the crown and summary of much of the best in Drayton's work. Here he departed from the conventional type of pastoral, even more than in the Shepherd's Garland; but to say that he sang of English rustic life would hardly be true: the sixth Nymphal, allowing for a few pardonable exaggerations by the competitors, is almost all English, if we except the names; so is the tenth with the same exception; the first and fourth might take place anywhere, but are not likely in any country; the second is more conventional; the fifth is almost, but not quite, English; the third, seventh, and ninth are avowedly classical in theme; while the eighth is a more delicate and subtle fairy poem than the Nymphidia. The fourth and tenth Nymphals are also touched with the sadder, almost satiric vein; the former inveighing against the English imitation of foreigners and love of extravagance in dress; while the tenth complains of the improvident and wasteful felling of trees in the English forests. This last Nymphal, though designedly an epilogue, is probably rather a warning than a despairing lament, even though we conceive the old satyr to be Drayton himself. As a whole the Nymphals show Drayton at his happiest and lightest in style and metre; at his moments of greatest serenity and even gaiety; an atmosphere of sunshine seems to envelope them all, though the sun sink behind a cloud in the last. His music now is that of a rippling stream, whereas in his earlier days he spoke weightier and more sonorous words, with a mouth of gold.

To estimate the poetical faculty of Drayton is a somewhat perplexing task; for, while rarely subtle, or rising to empyrean heights, he wrote in such varied styles, on such various themes, that the task, at first, seems that of criticizing many poets, not one. But through all his work runs the same eminently English spirit, the same honesty and clearness of idea, the same stolidity of purpose, and not infrequently of execution also; the same enthusiasm characterizes all his earlier, and much of his later work; the enthusiasm especially characteristic of Elizabethan England, and shown by Drayton in his passion for England and the English, in his triumphant joy in their splendid past, and his certainty of their future glory. As a poet, he lacked imagination and fine fury; he supplied their place by the airiest and clearest of fancies, by the strenuous labour of a great brain illumined by the steady flame of love for his country and for his lady. Mr. Courthope has said that he lacked loftiness and resolution of artistic purpose; without these, we ask, how could a man, not lavishly dowered with poetry in his soul, have achieved so much of it? It was his very fixity and loftiness of purpose, his English stubbornness and doggedness of resolution that enabled him to surmount so many obstacles of style and metre, of subject and thought. His two purposes, of glorifying his mistress and his friends, and of sounding England's glories past and future, while insisting on the dangers of a present decadence, never flagged or failed. All his poetry up to 1627 has this object directly or secondarily; and much after this date. Of the more abstract and universal aspects of his art he had not much conception; but he caught eagerly at the fashionable belief in the eternizing power of poetry; and had it not been that, where his patriotism was uppermost, he was deficient in humour and sense of proportion, he would have succeeded better: as it is, his more directly patriotic pieces are usually the dullest or longest of his works. He requires, like all other poets, the impulse of an absolutely personal and individual feeling, a moment of more intimate sympathy, to rouse him to his heights of song. Thus the Ballad of Agincourt is on the very theme of all patriotic themes that most attracted him; Virginian and other Voyages lay very close to his heart; and in certain sonnets to his lady lies his only imperishable work. Of sheer melody and power of song he had little, apart from his themes: he could not have sat down and written a few lark's or nightingale's notes about nothing as some of his contemporaries were able to do: he required the stimulus of a subject, and if he were really moved thereby he beat the music out. Only in one or two of the later Odes, and in the volumes of 1627 and 1630, does his music ever seem to flow from him naturally. Akin to this quality of broad and extensive workmanship, to this faculty of taking a subject and when writing, with all thought concentrated on it, rather than on the method of writing about it, is his strange lack of what are usually called 'quotations'. For this is not only due to the fact that he is little known; there are, besides, so few detached remarks or aphorisms that are separately quotable; so few examples of that curiosa felicitas of diction: lines like these,

Thy Bowe, halfe broke, is peec'd with old desire;
Her Bowe is beauty with ten thousand strings....

are rare enough. Drayton, in fact, comes as near controverting the statement Poeta nascitur, non fit, as any one in English literature: by diligent toil and earnest desire he won a place for himself in the second rank of English poets: through love he once set foot in the circle of the mightiest. Sincere he was always, simple often, sensuous rarely. His great industry, his careful study, and his great receptivity are shown in the unusual spectacle of a man who has sung well in the language of his youth, suddenly learning, in his age, the tongue spoken by the younger generation, and reproducing it with individuality and sureness of touch. It is in rhetoric, splendid or rugged, in argument, in plain statement or description, in the outline sketch of a picture, that Drayton excels; magic of atmosphere and colouring are rarely present. Stolidity is, perhaps, his besetting sin; yet it is the sign of a slow, not a dull, intellect; an intellect, like his heart, which never let slip what it had once taken to itself.

As a man Drayton would seem to have been an excellent type of the sturdy, clear-headed, but yet romantic and enthusiastic Englishman; gifted with much natural ability, sedulously increased by study; quietly humorous, self-restrained; and if temporarily soured by disappointment and the disjointed times, yet emerging at last into a greater serenity, a more unadulterated gaiety than had ever before characterized him. It is possible, but from his clear and sane balance of mind improbable, that many of his light later poems are due to deliberate self-blinding and self-deception, a walking in enchanted lands of the mind.

Of Drayton's three known portraits the earliest shows him at the age of thirty-six, and is now in the National Portrait Gallery. A look of quiet, speculative melancholy seems to pervade it; there is, as yet, no moroseness, no evidence of severe conflict with the world, no shadow of stress or of doubt. The second and best-known portrait shows us Drayton at the age of fifty, and was engraved by Hole, as a frontispiece to the poems of 1619. Here a notable change has come over the face; the mouth is hardened, and depressed at the corners through disappointment and disillusionment; the eyes are full of a pathos increased by the puzzled and perturbed uplift of the brows. Yet a stubbornness and tenacity of purpose invests the features and reminds us that Drayton is of the old and sound Elizabethan stock, 'on evil days though fallen.' Let it be remembered, that he was in 1613, when the portrait was taken, in more or less prosperous circumstances; it was the sad degeneracy, the meanness and feebleness of the generation around him, that chiefly depressed and embittered him. The final portrait, now in the Dulwich Gallery, represents the poet as a man of sixty-five; and is quite in keeping with the sunnier and calmer tone of his later poetry. It is the face of one who has not emerged unscathed from the world's conflict, but has attained to a certain calm, a measure of tranquillity, a portion of content, who has learnt the lesson that there is a soul of goodness in things evil. The Hole portrait shows him with long hair, small 'goatee' beard, and aquiline nose drawn up at the nostrils: while the National portrait shows a type of nose and beard intermediate between the Hole and the Dulwich pictures: the general contour of the face, though the forehead is broad enough, is long and oval. Drayton seems to have been tall and thin, and to have been very susceptible of cold, and therefore to have hated Winter and the North. He is said to have shared in the supper which caused Shakespeare's death; but his own verses breathe the spirit of Milton's sonnet to Cyriack Skinner, rather than that of a devotee of Bacchus.

He died in 1631, probably December 23, and was buried under the North wall of Westminster Abbey. Meres's opinion of his character during his early life is as follows: 'As Aulus Persius Flaccus is reported among al writers to be of an honest life and upright conuersation: so Michael Drayton, quem totics honoris et amoris causa nomino, among schollers, souldiours, Poets, and all sorts of people is helde for a man of uertuous disposition, honest conversation, and well governed cariage; which is almost miraculous among good wits in these declining and corrupt times, when there is nothing but rogery in villanous man, and when cheating and craftines is counted the cleanest wit, and soundest wisedome.' Fuller also, in a similar strain, says, 'He was a pious poet, his conscience having the command of his fancy, very temperate in his life, slow of speech, and inoffensive in company.'

A Chronology of Michael Drayton's Life and Works

1563	Drayton born at Hartshill, Warwickshire.
c. 1572	Drayton a page in the house of Sir Henry Goodere, at Polesworth.
c. 1574	Anne Goodere born
February, 1591	Drayton in London. Harmony of Church.
1593	Idea, the Shepherd's Garland. Legend of Peirs Gaveston.
1594	Ideas Mirrour. Matilda. Lucy Harrington becomes Countess of Bedford.
1595	Sir Henry Goodere the elder dies. Endimion and Phoebe, dedicated to Lucy Bedford.
1595-6	Anne Goodere married to Sir Henry Raynsford.
1596	Mortimeriados. Legends of Robert, Matilda, and Gaveston.
1597	England's Heroical Epistles.
1598	Drayton already at work on the Poly-Olbion.
1599	Epistles and Idea sonnets, new edition. (Date of Drayton portrait in National Portrait Gallery.)
1600	Sir John Oldcastle.
1602	New edition of Epistles and Idea.
1603	Drayton made an Esquire of the Bath, to Sir Walter Aston. To the Maiestie of King James. Barons' Wars.
1604	The Owle. A Pean Triumphall. Moyses in a Map of his Miracles.
1605	First collected edition of Poems. Another edition of Idea and Epistles.
1606	Poemes Lyrick and Pastorall. Odes. Eglogs. The Man in the Moone.
1607	Legend of Great Cromwell.
1608	Reprint of Collected Poems.
1609	Another edition of Cromwell.
1610	Reprint of Collected Poems.
1613	Reprint of Collected Poems. First Part of Poly-Olbion.
1618	Two Elegies in FitzGeoffrey's Satyrs and Epigrames.
1619	Collected Folio edition of Poems.
1620	Second edition of Elegies, and reprint of 1619 Poems.
1622	Poly-Olbion complete.
1627	Battle of Agincourt, Nymphidia, &c.

1630	Muses Elizium. Noah's Floud. Moses his Birth and Miracles. David and Goliah.
1631	Second edition of 1627 folio. Drayton dies December 23rd.
1636	Posthumous poem appeared in Annalia Dubrensia.
1637	Poems.

Michael Drayton – A Concise Bibliography

The Major Works

The Harmony of the Church (1591)
Idea, The Shepherd's Garland (1593)
Idea's Mirror (1594)
Peirs Gaveston (1593 or 1594)
Matilda (1594)
Endimion and Phoebe: Idea's Latmus (1595)
The Tragical Legend of Robert, Duke of Normandy (1596)
Mortimeriados (1596)
England's Heroicall Epistles (1597)
The First Part of the Life of Sir John Oldcastle (1600)
The Barons' Wars in the Reign of Edward II (1603)
The Owl (1604)
The Man in the Moon (1606)
The Legend of Thomas Cromwell, Earl of Essex (1607)
Poly-Olbion (1612 & 1622)
Idea (1619)
Pastorals: Containing Eclogues (1619)
Odes (1619)
The Battle of Agincourt (published 1627)
The Quest of Cynthia (published 1627)
Elegies Upon Sundry Occasions (1627)
Nymphidia, the Court of Fairy (1627)
The Shepherd's Sirena (1627)
Muses' Elysium (1630)
Moses' Birth and Miracles (1630)

www.ingramcontent.com/pod-product-compliance
Lightning Source LLC
Chambersburg PA
CBHW060142050426
42448CB00010B/2248